The Bill of Rights

The Bill of Rights

Politics, Religion, and the Quest for Justice

John Patterson

iUniverse, Inc.
New York Lincoln Shanghai

The Bill of Rights
Politics, Religion, and the Quest for Justice

iUniverse, Inc.

For information address:
iUniverse, Inc.
2021 Pine Lake Road, Suite 100
Lincoln, NE 68512
www.iuniverse.com

ISBN: 0-595-31398-1

Printed in the United States of America

CONTENTS

PREFACE

Suppose you lived in a country where you could be tried for a crime without the help of a defense attorney and where a member of the local police acted as the judge. Imagine in that same land that your home could be searched at any time without a court order.

What if you lived in a place where you had no right to speak out against a particular law or local ordinance? What if the government of this same country forced you to practice a certain religion or be punished by the loss of your job, imprisonment, or even torture?

What would you think about living in a country where only the military possessed weapons and the citizens had none? What if the leaders of that same nation could take away your private property without paying you fairly for it?

If these things existed in your nation, you would live in a police state. You would have no Bill of Rights. Sadly, many Americans have a poor understanding about where these God-given rights came from.

Most of world history is the story of people living under tyranny. It might have been under the potentates of Babylon, the pharaohs of Egypt, the warlords of Assyria, the conquerors of Greece, or the caesars of Rome.

While elements of the rule of law existed in the ancient world, raw power usually prevailed over people's rights. Ancient Israel had a few fine rulers in men like David, Josiah, and Jehoshaphat, but most of the kings of the Hebrews were not interested in human rights.

Later in history, Jesus Christ entered as the Savior and king. While he primarily proclaimed a kingdom that first started in the human spirit, the idea of government *defending* human rights rather than *trampling* on them can be derived from his teachings.

For hundreds of years after the time of Christ, many people lived under oppression from various sultans, tribal chiefs, and kings of both the pagan and civilized worlds. After a millennium, the idea of restraining the power of government came alive in Europe during the later middle ages. The signing of the Magna Carta in England was a crucial turning point.

The people of colonial America understood that there were limits to the power of the English Parliament and king. When they came to the conclusion that their rights were violated, they rebelled. This rebellion was a co-operative effort of many people and was based upon their understanding of human rights in English law that were developed over hundreds of years. After the Constitution was established, this tradition of rights was quickly adopted and became our Bill of Rights.

This book begins with the Magna Carta, moves to 14th century England, travels through the turmoil of 17th century England, lands in Colonial America, and ends with the debate over the Bill of Rights in our new nation.

It is a short work of history *about* the Bill of Rights. It is not an explanation of them. You will not be reading social or political philosophy. You will be reading about people and events. *Religion, politics, and the desire for justice will be presented to you as the driving forces behind the development of these rights.*

The following are the first ten amendments to the United States Constitution known as the *Bill of Rights:*

Article I. Congress shall make no law respecting an establishment of religion, or prohibiting the free exercise thereof; or abridging the freedom of speech, or of the press; or the right of the people peaceably to assemble, and to petition the Government for a redress of grievances.

Article II. A well-regulated militia, being necessary to the security of a free State, the right of the people to keep and bear arms, shall not be infringed.

Article III. No soldier shall, in time of peace be quartered in any house, without the consent of the owner, nor in time of war, but in a manner to be prescribed by law.

Article IV. The right of the people to be secure in their persons, houses, papers, and effects, against unreasonable searches and seizures, shall not be violated, and no warrants shall issue, but upon probable cause, supported by oath or affirmation, and particularly describing the place to be searched, and the persons or things to be seized.

Article V. No person shall be held to answer for a capital, or otherwise infamous crime, unless on a presentment or indictment of a Grand Jury, except in cases arising in the land or naval forces, or in the militia, when in actual service in time of war or public danger; nor shall any person be subject for the same offense to be put twice in jeopardy of life or limb; nor shall be compelled in any criminal case to be a witness against himself, nor be deprived of life, liberty,

or property, without due process of law; nor shall private property be taken for public use without just compensation.

Article VI. In all criminal prosecutions, the accused shall enjoy the right to a speedy and public trial, by an impartial jury of the State and district wherein the crime shall have been committed, which district shall have been previously ascertained by law, and to be informed of the nature and cause of the accusation; to be confronted with the witnesses against him; to have compulsory process for obtaining witnesses in his favor, and to have the assistance of counsel for his defense.

Article VII. In suits at common law, where the value in controversy shall exceed twenty dollars, the right of trial by jury shall be preserved, and no fact tried by a jury shall be otherwise reexamined in any court of the United States, than according to the rules of the common law.

Article VIII. Excessive bail shall not be required, nor excessive fines imposed, nor cruel and unusual punishments inflicted.

Article IX. The enumeration in the Constitution, of certain rights, shall not be construed to deny or disparage others retained by the people.

Article X. The powers not delegated to the United States by the Constitution, nor prohibited by it to the States, are reserved to the States respectively, or to the people.

THE MAGNA CARTA

The Magna Carta has been called the cornerstone of English liberty. It was the first document to challenge the king's power to tax his subjects and it seriously limited his authority.

Richard "the Lionhearted" was the king of England in the late 1100s. He was often away from the homeland because he was out fighting in the **crusades** or defending England's possessions in continental Europe.

His government raised two large sums of money for him, one to pay for a crusade to the Holy Land, and the other to buy his ransom after some opponents in Austria captured him. In 1199, Richard died during the siege of a castle in France. His brother **John** then became king (1199-1216). At that time, England held possession of large portions of territory in France. The French were starting to reclaim some of it under King Phillip Augustus, who won back Normandy in 1204. King John needed money to govern England *and* to fight in France, so he taxed the nobles to get it. The **barons** of England were not very happy with these taxes.

In 1213, a group of barons and church leaders met at St. Albans near London and wrote up a list of rights that they wanted the king to recognize. King John refused twice to agree to these terms. The nobles then decided to raise an army against him. Realizing that he could not defeat this force, John agreed to meet the barons at Runnymede on June 15, 1215. There he placed his seal on *The Magna Carta* (The Great Charter). This document restricted the power of the Crown to tax and issue fines. It also forced the king not to deny due process of law to any **freeman** in his realm. No one's property could unjustly be taken. No one could be imprisoned except by proper legal process or the judgment of people in the community. While *The Magna Carta* did not promote democracy, it was the first limitation of a king's powers by those who were being governed.

King John

King John pretended that all of this was an act of grace on his part toward his subjects. Nothing could have been further from the truth. John acted as he did because the barons threatened him with swords, spears, and arrows.

Religion was another aspect of the signing of the Magna Carta. **Pope Innocent III**, the most powerful of the medieval popes and the father of the **Inquisition**, wanted to strengthen the power of the **Roman Catholic Church.** In 1206, King John and the monastery of Canterbury had a dispute about who should be the Archbishop of England. Innocent stepped in to resolve the matter with his own choice, a man named **Stephen Langton.** John did not care for the pope's decision and decided to seize church lands and persecute some of the clergy. Pope Innocent responded by laying all England under a **papal interdict.**

For the next six years churches were closed, communion was not given, and the dead were buried in unconsecrated ground. In 1209, the pope **excommunicated** John, and his enemies received the blessing of the church as Crusaders. King John remained belligerent. He took more church property and funds from the abbeys. Innocent then incited the king of France, Phillip Augustus, to invade England under the papal banner. In 1213, John realized that he would probably be defeated and gave in to the demands of Innocent rather than risk an invasion by a French army.

At this point, one of the most amazing and selfish political turnarounds in history took place. John offered to make England a **fief** of the Papacy and pay homage to the pope as his feudal Lord. Innocent, who was very interested in expanding the Church's acquisitions, gladly accepted John's offer. He forgave John all of his past offenses and put him and the English people under his special protection. King John became a **vassal** of the pope. The tables were turned on John's enemies. The barons were now under pressure to submit to King John and the pope.

Pope Innocent III

However, the barons still had grievances that were not addressed. The English **Episcopacy** was also unhappy with this new subjection to Rome. The English Church had traditionally kept a certain amount of independence. While the English bishops felt it was their sacred duty to obey the Roman pontiff, they also believed that Rome could push things too far. Stephen Langton, the pope's choice to head the English Church, saw that Rome was being heavy handed and he became an opponent of Pope Innocent.

Langton forged an alliance of churchmen and barons who opposed King John and Pope Innocent. Meanwhile, John continued to lose the war on French soil. His demands for money made the barons hotter. An armed revolt was a possibility, but Archbishop Langton tempered their plans by suggesting a more moderate course.

John responded by taking the vow of a crusader for the pope. The barons rebelled. A few years earlier, they had opposed the excommunicated king. Now *they* were under a **papal bull** of excommunication. However, a great number of English church leaders supported these barons. Archbishop Langton did not want to see a civil war. He led the nobles on a course of presenting their demands upon ancient law and custom. The barons had also learned to think constructively. They proposed a system of government that would not be based upon the arbitrary rule of the king, but upon the idea of a system of checks and balances that would prevent tyranny. *The English barons moved forward in the dim light toward the constitutional principle that custom and law must stand above the king.*

The Magna Carta (The Great Charter)

On Monday morning of June 15th, the barons and the English churchmen collected themselves together on the great meadow at Runnymede. This was a bold move on their part. They suspected that the king would not forgive this humiliation, and if he ever had the chance, he would hunt them down for torture or execution. They had drawn up a document on parchment and kept their armed horseman well in the background to avoid the appearance of armed rebellion. Then King John, the pope's legate, and the king's small force arrived. The terms were laid out and the king accepted. The king and the barons agreed to the **Magna Carta.** Later on, John appealed to Pope Innocent for permission to repudiate his agreement with the barons, saying he was forced to sign it. Innocent agreed, but John died about a year later.

The Magna Carta is the foundation of human liberties developed in England and America. It was a medieval tool used by the less centralized powers (the barons) to control the more centralized powers of the king. The barons insisted that they had rights that the king could not violate. The Great Charter also helped the English Church keep its distance from the Church in Rome.

The Magna Carta established the principle in feudal times that the moral law of God was above the law of any particular ruler.

Excerpts from the Magna Carta

1. We have in the first place granted to God and by this our present charter....that the English Church shall be free and shall have its rights entire and its liberties inviolate....

8. No widow shall be forced to marry as long as she wishes to live without a husband....

9. Neither we [the king's government] nor our bailiffs [justice officials] will seize any land or revenue for any debt, so long as any of the chattels [moveable personal property] are sufficient to repay the debt....If the chief debtor, having nothing with which to pay, defaults in payment, the sureties [people who guarantee the debt] shall be responsible for the debt....

13. The city of London shall have all its ancient liberties and free customs, both by land and by water. Besides, we will and grant that all the other cities, boroughs, towns, and ports shall have all their liberties and free customs.

17. Common Pleas shall not follow our [the king's] court, but shall be held in a definite place.

20. A freeman shall be amerced [punished by a fine] for a small offence only according to the degree of the offence, saving his contentment. A merchant shall be amerced in the same way, saving his merchandise....and none of the aforesaid amercements [fines] shall be imposed except by the oaths of good men from the neighborhood.

21. Earls and barons shall be amerced [fined] only by their peers, and only according to the degree of their misdeed.

23. No man shall be detained to make bridges on riverbanks, except such as by right and ancient custom ought to do so.

29. No constable or other bailiff of ours, shall take grain or other chattels [moveable property] of anyone without immediate payment therefore in money, unless the seller allows him to postpone payment.

30. No sheriff or bailiff of ours, nor any other person, shall take the horses or carts of any freeman for carrying service, except by the will of that freeman.

31. Neither we [the king's government] nor our bailiffs will take someone else's wood for [repairing] castles or for doing any other work of ours, except by the will of him to whom the wood belongs.

38. No bailiff shall henceforth put anyone to law by merely bringing suit [against him] without trustworthy witnesses for this purpose.

39. No freeman shall be captured or imprisoned, deprived of property, outlawed, exiled, or in any way destroyed....except by the lawful judgment of his peers or by the law of the land.

41. All merchants may safely and securely go away from England, come to England, stay in and go through England, by land or by water, for buying and selling under right and ancient customs....

52. If anyone, without the lawful judgment of his peers, has been deprived of lands, castles, liberties, or rights, we will at once restore them to him. And if a dispute arises in this connection,

then let the matter be decided by the judgment of twenty-five barons....

61. ...for God, for the improvement of our kingdom, and for [the calming] of the conflict between us and our barons, we have granted all these liberties....and have granted them the following security: namely that the barons shall elect twenty-five barons of the kingdom, whomever they please, who to the best of their ability should observe, hold, and cause to be observed the peace and liberties that we have granted to them and have confirmed by this our present charter; so that if we....or any of our ministers....transgresses any article....four of those barons shall come to us....to explain to us the wrong, asking without delay we cause this wrong to be redressed. [If] we do not redress the wrong within forty days....the four barons shall refer that case to the rest of the twenty-five barons, and those twenty-five barons with the rest of the community of the entire country, shall distress and injure us in all ways possible—namely by capturing our castles, lands, and possessions and in all ways that they can (except us and our children)—until they secure redress according to their own decision. And when redress has been made, they shall be obedient to us as they were before.

Glossary

Barons—Men in the Middle Ages who were feudal tenants (in charge of lands) of the king or a high-ranking lord. They were also called *great vassals*. Barons could grant land to lesser vassals who had authority over smaller areas.

Crusades—Military expeditions taken by European Roman Catholics from the 11th to the 13th centuries for the purpose of taking back the Holy Land from the Moslems.

Episcopacy—A system of church government by bishops.

Excommunicate—A church's act of forbidding a person (or people) from partaking in Communion and the other sacraments. They were cut off from the church.

Fief—Lands, homes, supply houses, equipment, etc. that were held by a baron (under a lord). The baron had serfs work on the land to produce crops and other necessities for the lord who owned it.

Freeman—A person not in slavery or bondage who had full possession of political and civil rights.

Inquisition—A general tribunal of the Roman Catholic Church during the 13th century for the purpose of discovering heresy (teachings the church considered to be unorthodox) and suppressing and punishing those who were considered heretics.

Papal Bull—An official document or decree from the pope.

Papal Interdict—A pope's pronouncement that a parish or territory was to be excluded from the church's sacraments and privileges.

Roman Catholic Church—The system of faith and practice in Western Christianity that is headed by the pope in Rome. A group of churches in a given area is called a diocese, and is governed by a bishop. This form of the Christian religion emphasizes the sacramental life. Its members are encouraged to have a high view of its religious and eccle-siastical authority.

Vassal—A person who held land (a fief) under a lord. A baron was a great vassal. Vassals performed military and other duties in return for the protection of the lord. A vassal is not to be confused with a serf (or peasant), who was the lowest field worker in the feudal system.

PLAGUE, POWER, AND REFORM

The Four Horseman of the Apocalypse

The Plague

In 1334, Europe was invaded by the most vicious pestilence to strike the Western World. **The Black Death** entered Europe through the Crimea, and in twenty years between one-fourth and one-third of its population was destroyed. Death was quick and awful. Chills, fever, and headache led to the swelling of the lymph glands. Spots of blood turned black under the skin. Then came diarrhea. After these terrible symptoms came open sores, followed by delirium (sometimes insanity) and death. All of this would happen within one week. The cities and the clergy were especially hard hit. Panic-stricken people fled to the countryside to avoid the contagion. This epidemic was probably a **bubonic plague** carried by fleas from rats. It had a devastating impact on the psyche of the people.

Winston Churchill wrote, "The character of the pestilence was appalling. The disease itself, with its frightful symptoms, the swift onset...the delirium, the insanity which attended its triumph...stunned, and for a time, destroyed the life and faith of the world."

The Roman Catholic Church, the sole religious institution of Europe, was also smitten by the Plague. This effect was temporal and spiritual. While kings were powerful, the church was understood to be in charge of eternal human souls, a far more important matter. The Plague, however, did not respect the church. The church's priests and monks actually had a higher death rate than the rest of the population. The pope retreated to the interior of his palace and no one was allowed to enter. Many clergymen fled like everyone else. The church could not stop the Black Death. People realized that no power, either religious or political, provided safety for them if they were caught by this pestilence. The disease was believed to be the wrath of God. Many people thought that one of the **Four Horsemen of the Apocalypse** was riding against Europe. In Germany, people wandered through the streets whipping one another with metal tipped scourges. These *Flagellant Processions* were performed in hopes of warding off God's wrath.

The Black Death hit England as hard as the rest of Europe. But in time, the Plague subsided. As it receded and recoveries became more frequent, physical disease gave way to political and religious agitations in Britain. *The Plague did affect the minds and hearts of people, as well as their bodies. In its own way, the Plague smashed the idea that church and state were all powerful institutions. In England, the concept of people having rights and liberties probably moved forward even during this dark period.*

Under **King Edward III** (1312-1377), the power of **Parliament** developed. The separation of the **House of Commons** and the **House of Lords** appeared. While the Parliament was submissive to the king, Edward accepted formal petitions from the Commons as a basis for future laws. The Lords came to regard themselves as natural counselors of the Crown.

The English people developed strong feelings against Papal agents in England and criticism of the Church grew louder. Churchmen had more wealth than the common people who had undergone the severe economic trials brought about by the Plague. The church was also trying to get rid of the nobility from public offices. King Edward was old and failing, and *the barons were coming forth again to reclaim their power.* **John of Gaunt** became the leader of the Lords and conducted a political campaign against the church.

One of the reasons for the decline of the clergy's prestige was *the increase in lay people's literacy.* The cost of books went down and education increased. When the common people began to be able to read the Bible, they realized that some of their priests were not living according to the standards of Jesus Christ and the Apostles. The horrors of the late middle ages, primarily war and plague, drove people to seek the Lord outside the walls of the institutional church. Acts of external devotion such as barefooted processions were one means of attempting to please God. Whippings or flagellations were also practiced. **Indulgences** were sought after and paid for.

Mysticism also played a role in the 1300s. In Germany and England, mystics sought union with God through contemplation, "detachment," and other spiritual exercises. Most of them were priests, nuns, and hermits. As the movement spread into the lay world, it took on not so much an ecstatic private union with God, but a communion with God in the daily affairs of life.

Wyclif and the Lollards

Religious protest also developed in the 14th century. The man who led the protest was **John Wyclif.** This Oxford scholar attracted attention in both politics and religion. He was indignant at the corruption in the Church and saw it as an institution that had distorted the truth of Christianity. He taught that the king and the pope had different spheres of responsibility and that it was the duty of the king to roll back the excess material wealth and extravagances of some church leaders by taking their wealth and replacing corrupt priests. Wyclif wanted to reduce the temporal (worldly) power of the Church and purify its spiritual power.

John Wyclif

John of Gaunt and the English aristocracy originally supported Wyclif. Gaunt and Wyclif formed an alliance in 1377. Wyclif concerned himself with the abuses of the Church and Gaunt concerned himself with power in the Parliament. The Roman Catholic Episcopate was not pleased with either and they charged Wyclif with heresy. Wyclif faded in the political realm but his influence in religious and moral reforms increased. He organized bands of followers called **Lollards** who spread doctrines of holiness and poverty throughout the countryside. He also wrote tracts and taught that the sacred scriptures could be learned by common men and applied to everyday life. The Lollards taught that good Christians should shun the corrupt Church, study the Bible, and rely on spiritually enlightened consciences. Wyclif's influence was great, and the Lollards grew through the end of the fourteenth century. While they did fade away in the next century due to persecution, their beliefs and practices remained alive and contributed to the Protestant Reformation in the late 1500s.

The England of the 14th century was shaken up religiously, politically, and culturally. *Plague, the modest beginnings of Parliament, and more freedom of thought about church and state were slowly moving the English speaking peoples toward representative government and a bill of rights.*

The Lollards

This religious society in 14th and 15th century England followed the teachings of Oxford professor and theologian John Wyclif. Those in it practiced simplicity of life, helping the sick, and preaching the gospel. They criticized the wealth, pomp, and worldliness of the Church. The Lollards taught that the Bible was the ultimate authority for faith and life. They also opposed the Church's doctrine of transubstantiation and the sacrament of confession. The Lollards promoted reading the scriptures and taught a Christian faith that was built on living out the gospel. Nicknamed "Poor Priests," they wore long russet gowns and carried staffs as they went about preaching in the villages of England.

In 1399, Henry IV came to the throne and declared himself their enemy. Under Henry and Thomas Arundel, the Archbishop of Canterbury, the Lollards were persecuted to the point of extinction. Their leaders were tortured and imprisoned. Many were burned at the stake. Their numbers diminished dramatically over the next hundred years as they were persecuted under Henry V and Henry VI. However, their ideas lived on and paved the way for the Reformation.

Renaissance and Reformation

These two movements spread across Europe during the 15th and 16th centuries. The **Renaissance** was a revival of the literature, architecture, and philosophies found in classical Greece and Rome. There was also a renewed interest in art and science.

The thinkers of the Renaissance wanted to replace the old scholastic model of learning with its emphasis on logic and metaphysics. Their new model involved the study of medicine, science, history, language, and ethics. They preferred understanding human concerns rather than the dry and rigid teachings of Thomas Aquinas. Some leaders in this new way of thinking argued for man's excellence because only he could possess the knowledge of God. Others simply stressed man's need to master his own fate and live a happy life.

Leonardo da Vinci was the ultimate Renaissance man. This naturalist and vegetarian excelled at art, science, engineering, inventions, and medicine. He even performed autopsies. The artist **Raphael** (1483-1520) depicted human beings with noble and spiritual qualities. Michelangelo became renown for his painting of the Sistine Chapel that included scenes of God creating Adam and Eve, the drunkenness of Noah after the Flood, and the Last Judgment. His figures had an element of ancient Greek artistry in them.

In politics, **Niccolo Machiavelli** (1469-1527) wrote *The Prince*. This book described the policies of government that were based on the realities of human greed and the desire for power. He was a cynic who believed that rulers should not be concerned with high moral principles, but should use whatever means were necessary to accomplish the goals of safety and security for their countries.

The most outstanding literary man of the Renaissance was **Erasmus.** Born in Rotterdam, Holland in 1467, he came to view the Roman Catholic Church as incompetent and corrupt. However, he never went as far as Martin Luther in denouncing the church, and he remained within it. Erasmus believed in a simple faith and Christian charity based on the teachings of Christ and practiced by the early church. He upheld the power of reason to overcome superstition, ignorance, and hate.

In 1498, a republic was established in Florence, Italy. It lasted less than fifteen years. There was little effort to overturn European monarchies during this period, but minds and hearts were open to change. *The Renaissance was an age in which the people of Europe became interested in broad human concerns. This included government. More and more, men were questioning whether or not their leaders were doing the right thing.*

The Renaissance had more influence in continental Europe than it did in England. But where it lacked influence in the English world, the **Reformation** filled the gap. While the warm-tempered **Martin Luther** gets most of the credit for the Reformation, English pre-reformers like **John Wyclif** and **William Tyndale** did much for the religious and political liberties of the English-speaking world. The reserved **John Calvin** was certainly more influential than Luther when it came to shaping political and religious ideas in England.

After ending his humanist education in Paris, Calvin went to Basel, Switzerland where he wrote *The Institutes of the Christian Religion* in 1536. Calvin later settled in Geneva where he established a systematic approach to Christian living that involved church, state, private institutions, and public morals. Under Calvin, works of charity were improved and civil government was considered a ministry under God.

Calvin blended theocratic and democratic principles. *He taught that hereditary monarchy was not in accordance with liberty.* He wrote, "It is much more endurable to have leaders who are chosen and elected…and who acknowledge themselves subject to the laws, than to have a prince who gives utterance without reason. Let those to whom God has given liberty use it…as a…treasure that cannot be prized enough."

Calvin's ideas were transported from Geneva to London, and his views on religious and civil freedoms started to blossom during the reign of Queen Elizabeth. *The Calvinist wing of the Reformation found a home in the English cities and towns. The Reformation was political as well as religious. It was only a matter of time before the established church and the monarchy were on the defensive. Soon enough, English leaders would start to demand that the king bow to the rights of the people and their Parliament.*

Glossary

Bubonic Plague—A contagious disease caused by a bacterium carried by fleas from infected rats. One of the symptoms was bubos, or swelling of the lymph glands.

Four Horsemen of the Apocalypse—Riders of divine judgment in the sixth chapter of the Book of Revelation. They represent Conquest, War, Famine, and Death. The horses are white, red, black, and pale.

Indulgences—Roman Catholic Church teaching in which a person can have their punishment for sin in purgatory removed or reduced by doing acts sanctioned by the Church.

Humanism—An intellectual and cultural movement in the Middle Ages based on the study of the classical cultures of Greece and Rome. It emphasized the nature, dignity, qualities, and ideals of man.

Parliament—The national legislative body of Great Britain composed of a *House of Commons* and a *House of Lords.*

Purgatory—In Roman Catholic Church doctrine, the place where a person's spirit goes if they have died in a state of God's grace. It is a place of temporary punishment for sins before they enter heaven.

Renaissance—The great revival of learning, architecture, art, and literature in Europe from the 14th through the 16th centuries. The classical cultures of Greece and Rome were its sources of inspiration.

Reformation—The 16th century religious movement that initially intended to reform the Roman Catholic Church but ended up in establishing Protestant churches. It was based on the sacred scriptures and the desire to recover a simple faith from the apostolic and early church eras.

Scholastic (Scholasticism)—The system of learning in Medieval universities from the 10th to the 15th centuries. It was based on the philosophy of Aristotle, the writings of the early Christian fathers, and the authority of tradition.

THE GROWTH OF LIBERTY IN ENGLAND

The Defeat of the Spanish Armada

In July of 1588, King Phillip of Spain sent about 130 naval vessels to invade England. He did this for both political and religious reasons. Since his Protestant subjects in the Netherlands revolted with the aid of the English, Phillip realized that he had to master England first. The Spanish king was also angry at the way English privateers ("sea dogs") were attacking Spanish treasure ships and raiding Spanish towns in the Americas. He wanted to conquer England and re-establish Roman Catholicism there, partly because Elizabeth I persecuted the Catholics.

The plan was to send the invincible Armada up the English Channel and land an invasion force on British shores. The fleet was sighted off the English coast on July 29. Elizabeth gave a stirring speech to her troops in the field waiting for the invasion. But Spain never landed any troops. An English fleet commanded by Admiral Lord Charles Howard intercepted the Armada near Plymouth. The famous privateer Sir Francis Drake served as Vice-Admiral. For the next week,

Howard's smaller, faster, and more maneuverable ships attacked the Spanish in various battles off the English coast. The Spanish fleet was on the defensive but not broken. Then, as they anchored near Calais, France, the British struck a decisive blow. Admiral Howard set some ships on fire and sailed them at the Spanish Fleet. Confusion broke up the Spanish formation. At the Battle of Gravelines (also a French port) on August 8, the English defeated the Spanish. The damaged Spanish fleet tried to sail back to Spain through the English Channel but was forced to turn north and sail around Scotland because of bad winds. The fleet encountered more smashing winds in the North Sea. Only 67 of the original 130 ships made it back to Spain. Many of them returned in bad shape.

While the war between the two countries did not end for six more years, the victory by the English at sea was monumental. The Protestant faith was secured as the country's religion. English nationalism rose to high tide. *Constitutional liberty and the rights of English subjects started blossoming without the interference of a continental monarch.* The British navy was established as the backbone of England's defense and this naval power also meant that she would become dominant in North America in future years.

Past Profile

- Born in London, 1533
- Raised as a Protestant
- Becomes queen in 1558
- Re-establishes the Anglican Church
- Consents to the execution of Mary, Queen of Scots in 1587
- Her Royal Navy defeats the Spanish Armada in 1588
- Never Marries
- Constitutional liberty makes some progress during her reign
- Dies, 1603

Elizabeth I

The beginning of the 17th century was the end of the Elizabethan Age. **Queen Elizabeth** made a huge impact as England's ruler from 1558 to 1603. She was the daughter of Henry VIII and Anne Boleyn. She succeeded the infamous **Bloody Mary**. Queen Mary left Elizabeth a war with France to resolve, a dilapidated treasury, and a legacy of religious persecution against Protestants and **Dissenters**. Elizabeth ended the war, corrected English financial problems, and attempted to solve the religious question by re-establishing the **Anglican Church** as the state religion. Her record of religious tolerance was mixed. During her reign, many exiled Protestants returned from Geneva desiring reform. They wanted to see "papist superstition" removed from Anglican worship. Even though she was a Protestant, Elizabeth kept their influence in the Church to a minimum. These Calvinists (called **Puritans**) then turned their attention to Parliament, where they became a formidable minority. When they could not gain official positions in the established Church, they took advantage of lectureships that were given to them by some of the nobles. Their passion and devotion made the Puritans the most dynamic religious force in England at that time. They criticized the compromises that the Elizabethan Anglican Church made with Roman Catholicism. The queen kept the controversy from boiling over by practicing pragmatic politics and persecuting some of her opponents. She was able to control Parliament, but its influence continued to grow. The power of Parliament was to be felt in a much greater way during the rule of the next English monarch, **King James I**, whom Henry IV of France called, "the wisest fool in Christendom."

Past Profile

James I

- Born, 1566
- Son of Mary, Queen of Scots
- Becomes King in 1603
- Promotes "divine right of kings" theory
- Jamestown, Virginia named after him
- The King James Bible bears his name
- Although officially Protestant, he favors Catholics and harasses Dissenters
- Alienates Parliament
- Parliamentary resistance against him grows
- Dies, 1625

King James I

James I was a pompous and arrogant king. In a speech to Parliament in 1609, he declared that "kings are justly called gods, for they exercise a manner of resemblance of divine power on earth." This kind of belief about monarchy called the **divine right of kings** was prevalent during that time. *However, the English people did not forget the Magna Carta, which put limits on the power of the king.*

King James antagonized many people. He tried methods of taxation that were not approved by Parliament. When the leaders of that body protested, he dissolved the two Houses. He interfered with business by granting monopolies to favored companies. James also made peace with Spain and entered into marriage alliances favorable to Roman Catholic rulers. This upset the Anglican majority.

While the **Elizabethan Compromise** on the religious question brought the Reformation in England to a close, the more radical **Protestants** were not happy. They believed the Anglican Church was still too much like the Roman Catholic

Church. These Puritans separated into two factions. One group favored the purification of the Anglican church of all traces of "popish" ritual. Another group preferred to withdraw from the Anglican fold and establish separate congregations of worship. They were known as **Separatists** and later became famous in American history as the Pilgrims. Many of the Puritans opposed the episcopal system of church government, especially when the king appointed the bishops. James I thought that this opposition was disloyal and regarded the Puritans as traitors whom he was willing to "harry out of the land."

In 1605, a small group of Roman Catholics organized the **Gunpowder Plot.** Their design was to blow up the Parliament building while the king and the legislators were in it. This plot was discovered, and Parliament passed stringent laws against Catholics that James did not enforce.

Sir Edward Coke and the Petition of Right

Sir Edward Coke

From 1611 to 1621, James ruled without Parliament. However, a new champion was found in a man named **Sir Edward Coke.** He was appointed as chief

justice and had a great respect for the **common law** and the people's basic liberties. He was a defender of the position of lawyers and judges, and had a significant impact on the development of the concept called judicial review. Coke
(pronounced *cook*) believed that executive or parliamentary law that was against
common right and reason should be controlled by common law.

In 1616, Coke was dismissed from his position as Chief Justice of the King's
Bench. In 1620, at the age of 69, he was elected to the **House of Commons** and
embarked upon a new and important role as a lawmaker. The efforts to restrain
the power of the monarchy now shifted from the judicial to the parliamentary
realm. Coke was the great influence in all of this. The growing struggle between
Parliament and the king came to a head in 1628. At this time, a new **Stuart**
monarch came to the throne. **Charles I** came to power in 1625. During his first
three years, this king made some serious attacks on the liberties of the people.
Charles I forced a loan on the **gentry** and those who refused to pay were punished. Judges who refused to enforce it were dismissed. Men were sent to prison
by the command of the king and were not allowed out on bail. The men of the
House of Commons had to decide what to do about the situation.

*Sir Edward Coke declared that it was the law of the land that mattered, not the
arbitrary rule of the king.* In 1628, Parliament passed a declaration called the
Petition of Right. This petition said the king had no authority to imprison people arbitrarily. It challenged the king's authority to tax without the consent of
Parliament. It also stated that the king had no right to station soldiers in people's
homes during peacetime. *Later on, men of colonial America would follow Coke's
example of resistance to English laws that they thought were unjust.*

Excerpts from the 1628 Petition of Right

The second great charter of English liberty (after the Magna Carta) was the
Petition of Right. This work was mostly the creation of Sir Edward Coke. He was
followed later on by men like John Adams and Patrick Henry, leaders in the
American Revolution. In response to the serious attacks against the liberties of
Englishmen by King Charles I, the House of Commons passed this declaration of
rights in 1628. It was *not* an announcement of a new set of rights. It was a state-
ment by Parliament that the king must honor the traditional rights of the English
people.

> …it is declared and enacted that no freeman may be taken or impris-
> oned, be deprived of his liberties…, or be outlawed, exiled, or in any
> manner destroyed, but by the lawful judgment of his peers, or by the
> law of the land.

...no person should be compelled to make any loan to the king against his will..., and they should not be compelled to contribute any tax not set by common consent in parliament.

...great companies of soldiers and marines have been dispersed into various counties of the realm, and the inhabitants have been compelled to keep them in their houses against their wills, and against the laws and customs of the realm....and that your majesty be pleased to remove the said soldiers and marines, that your people may not be so burdened in time to come.

...many of your subjects have been imprisoned as of late without any cause showed..., they were brought before your justices, no cause was certified [by their jailors], and yet were returned back to several prisons, without being charged with anything to which they might make an answer according to the law...No freeman is to be imprisoned or detained, in any such manner as is mentioned.

In short, the petition declares these rights of the people:
- *No* short-term imprisonment or detention without a legal accusation (habeas corpus)
- *No* long-term imprisonment without a trial by jury
- *No* forced loans or taxes without the consent of Parliament
- *No* stationing of soldiers in the homes of citizens during peacetime

The Puritans

The Puritans started out as a movement in the later half of the 16th century. Their purpose was to reform (or purify) the Church of England beyond what Queen Elizabeth had done. Their political and religious influence grew during the first half of the 17th century (1600-1650). Theologically, the Puritans believed in **Calvinism.** Named after the reformer John Calvin, this was the doctrine that God chose to eternally save *some* people while all others would be lost. Calvinists taught that the conversion experience was the way in which a person could have some indication of this choice by God.

Various groups of Puritans developed both in England and America. Some accepted the **episcopacy** of the Church of England. Others demanded a **presbyterian** form of church rule. In New England, **congregationalism** became the model for church government.

The **Pilgrims** were the first group of Puritans to come to America. They were **separatists** who believed that the Church of England was too corrupt for them to participate in. Other Puritans arrived later who did not share these separatist views. In time, most Puritans left the English Church for the congregational system they developed.

The Puritan's influence grew dramatically during the reigns of James I and Charles I. They challenged the monarchy on both religious and civil matters. When Charles' agents Archbishop Laud and the Earl of Strafford attempted to suppress the Puritans (and Parliament), they were thrown into the Tower and executed, with Charles signing their death warrants against his own wishes.

Their political views on the rights of Parliament (and the common people) against the Crown were crucial in the development of the Bill of Rights both in England (1689) and America (1791).

In America, Puritans Thomas Hooker and Roger Williams left the Massachusetts Bay Colony for religious and political convictions to form their own colonies in Connecticut and Rhode Island.

Important figures in Puritanism were: **John Milton**—author of *Paradise Lost.* **John Bunyan**—author of *Pilgrims Progress.* **Oliver Cromwell**—*Lord Protector* during the English Commonwealth. **John Owen, Cotton Mather, Increase Mather**—theologians. **John Lilburne**—political radical and head of the *Levellers.* **John Pym**—leader of Parliament during the English Civil War.

The Puritan Revolution

Charles I, just like his father James, was a strong believer in the divine right of kings. Parliament didn't share his view. Charles did not like Parliament restricting his power with the *Petition of Right* and he resorted to other means of oppression. He compelled some of the wealthier **burghers** to apply for knighthood and pay high fees for the title. Judges were instructed to increase fines. **Monopolies** were sold at high prices. One of Charles' most unpopular measures was the collection of *ship money* in the inland counties as well as in the seacoast towns. Traditionally, the seaport towns contributed ships and money to the royal navy. But Charles wanted to expand this assessment to the rest of the country. Some people refused to pay and the king decided to prosecute them. A **squire** named John Hampden who wouldn't pay the levy was brought into court and convicted. He became a hero and a symbol of resistance to the Crown.

Charles also antagonized many people in religious matters. He appointed **William Laud** as **Archbishop of Canterbury**. Laud was a **High Church Anglican.** The Puritans and some **Low Church Anglicans** detested him. Laud used the Court of High Commission to look into the religious beliefs of both the nobles and the commoners. He persecuted the more radical Protestants and his tactics reminded the English people of the Inquisition. Archbishop Laud also angered the sabbatarian Puritans by authorizing public games on Sunday. In 1637, the archbishop attempted to impose *The Book of Common Prayer* and the Episcopal system on the Scottish Presbyterians. The result was armed rebellion by the Scots.

In 1640, the king called for Parliament to hold session (after eleven years of its absence) in order to raise money for a war against the Scots. Led by **John Pym,** Parliament issued its own demands. This **Long Parliament** abolished the Court of High Commission and impeached the king's chief ministers, Archbishop Laud and the Earl of Strafford. They were arrested, sent to the Tower, and executed.

In 1642, Parliament asserted its authority over county militias and declared that its authority was sovereign. The king was no longer an absolute ruler, but acted as the "king in Parliament." Charles would not stand for this and marched into the House of Commons with his guard in an attempt to arrest five parliamentary leaders, but they escaped. He then went to Oxford to raise an army. Parliament decided to raise its own. Thus, the English Civil War began.

Also known as the *Puritan Revolution,* the coalition against the king was composed of Puritans, Presbyterians, Parliamentarians, small landowners, tradesman, and manufacturers. They were known as the *Roundheads,* because they cut their hair short and did not follow the fashion of longer hair and curls for men. Their first aim was to negotiate peace with Charles. The goal was to limit his power constitutionally and reform the Church of England along Protestant lines. The members of the king's party were called *Cavaliers*. Nobles, large landowners, professional soldiers, Catholics, and staunch Anglicans made up this group. Also called Royalists, they had the advantage at first because of their military experience.

In 1644, the newly appointed Puritan lieutenant general, **Oliver Cromwell**, led the Parliamentary forces to victory over the king at the Battle of Marston Moor. In this battle, Cromwell and his troops earned the name *Ironsides*. In 1645, the reorganized *New Model Army* was sent to the field under **Sir Thomas Fairfax.** Cromwell became a cavalry commander. At the Battle of Naseby on June 14, Cromwell's right wing of the cavalry assaulted the king's forces and the Royalists were broken. In 1646, after other defeats, King Charles surrendered.

However, division broke out in Parliament. The majority were **Presbyterians** who wanted to restore Charles to the throne under a limited monarchy with Presbyterianism as the state religion of England. But a strong minority of Puritans were **Separatists** and Independents. They insisted on religious toleration for all Protestants. Oliver Cromwell was their leader. The minority had significant power because of its alliance with the military.

King Charles saw the opportunity to take advantage of this strife and renewed the war in 1648. The campaign didn't last long. The king's alliance with the Scots and the Irish did not help. Cromwell crushed the Scots at the battle of Preston in August. Within six months, Charles I was captured. The Roundheads called him "a man of blood." On January 30, 1649, he was beheaded in front of his palace. By all accounts he died a brave death. Bringing a king to trial and executing him was unique in history. It was even amazing. *By doing this, Cromwell and his followers ended the concept known as the divine right of kings. The execution of King Charles was an act that made it clear that the rights and liberties of the English people had to be respected even by the king.*

Cromwell's rule began with controversy. Many Englishmen were offended by the execution of the king. He and his allies threw 143 Presbyterians out of the House of Commons. About 60 members remained in what became known as the **Rump Parliament.** After the execution of Charles, the House of Lords was abolished and the new state was called a **Commonwealth.**

The Independent faction controlled this new government. The weakened Rump Parliament continued, but the real action occurred in a *Council of State* that had 41 members. Cromwell dominated both of these bodies since he had the loyalty of the army. Essentially what Cromwell established was a military dictatorship. This became known as the *Protectorate.*

Cromwell put the counties under the authority of "major generals." He also brought reforms to the courts and made the system of taxation more reasonable. He and the Independent Puritans wanted a "godly" government. Theaters were closed and dress codes were enforced. These actions were not popular. Parliament was inexperienced and inept. Many of those who were in it were idealists, ideologues, or simply corrupt men who wanted to enrich themselves with the confiscated wealth of their opponents.

In 1653, Cromwell marched a detachment of troops into Parliament and dispersed it. He established himself as military ruler under a constitution drafted by members of the army. It was called the *Instrument of Government*. Cromwell became the *Lord Protector* for life. However, he died in 1658. His son Richard took his place, but only held power for about eight months. England had become weary of the rigor of Cromwell's rule. Royalists despised the Independent Puritans. Presbyterians didn't care for them either. Republicans hated the military rule of Cromwell. Catholics and Anglicans were upset that their acts of worship were considered criminal. A new era was about to begin.

Liberator or Dictator?

Oliver Cromwell

Few men in English history have inspired more love and more hatred than Oliver Cromwell. Cromwell was born and educated in

Huntingdon. He was taught by Thomas Beard, an outspoken Puritan who wanted to purify England's national church of its Roman Catholic elements. He furthered his education at Sidney Sussex College and then returned to Huntingdon to manage his father's estate. From there, he became a Member of Parliament from 1628–1629. In the 1630s, Cromwell had a religious experience or conversion. From that time on, he was an intense Christian.

Military Career

Oliver Cromwell returned to Parliament in 1640 as the conflict between King Charles I and the Puritans reached a crisis. Civil war broke out in 1642 between the Puritan dominated Parliament and the Crown. Cromwell raised a regiment of cavalry to fight on the side of the Puritans. Although he had no military experience, he gained a reputation as a good commander during the early part of the war. Cromwell was quick to understand that religious passion could produce a fighting spirit that won battles. In 1644, Cromwell was made a lieutenant general. In that same year, he led Parliamentary forces to victory in the crucial battle of Marston Moor. It was there that he and his soldiers earned the nickname *Ironsides*.

In 1645, Cromwell was appointed cavalry commander in the reorganized New Model Army under Sir Thomas Fairfax. Christian commitment was an important part of this fighting force. At the battle of *Naseby*, Cromwell's leadership was decisive as King Charles' army was defeated. In this battle, Cromwell commanded the right wing of the Parliamentary cavalry. They beat back and broke the Royalists, bringing the first phase of the civil war to a close. Oliver Cromwell said that he had a great assurance of victory " because God would, by things that are nothing, bring to nothing, the things that are."

Negotiations with the king soon broke down and the Parliament split into two factions, Presbyterians and Independents. Cromwell and the army sided with the Independents. The Presbyterians favored their own national church and the Independents favored religious toleration. During this time, the king formed an alliance with the Scots, and renewed the civil war.

Oliver Cromwell's forces crushed the Scots at Preston in August of 1648. The army then purged the Parliament of Presbyterians in

December. A minority of Cromwell's supporters took over and became known as the *Rump Parliament*.

Lord Protector

Charles I was captured, convicted of treason, and beheaded. Parliament continued with the support of Cromwell and the army. In 1653, Cromwell disbanded the Parliament by military force, accusing it of being corrupt. The *Protectorate* was established and Cromwell became the military dictator of a government that was supposed to be a **republic** but was actually an **oligarchy**. Levellers, Presbyterians, and Royalists opposed him. Although he avoided the title of king, Cromwell became known as the Lord Protector. On February 4th, 1658, Cromwell disbanded the final Parliament during his military rule.

During the *Protectorate*, religious freedom grew while political opposition was stifled. Cromwell did not want any religious sect to gain power over others. He remarked, "Is there not a strange itch upon the spirits of men? Nothing will satisfy them unless they can press the finger upon their brethren's consciences to pinch them there." Cromwell felt it was his duty to prevent this. He did not want a state church that was either Anglican or Presbyterian. He was an Independent Puritan and the Independents were more of a confederation than a denomination.

During Cromwell's rule, Jews returned to England for the first time in over 300 years. Within the bounds of Protestantism, individual rights to practice any form of Christianity were protected (Roman Catholicism was not tolerated, mostly for political reasons). Cromwell encouraged, "If the poorest Christian, the most mistaken Christian, shall desire to live peaceably and quietly under you; I say if any desire but to live a life of godliness and honesty, let him be protected."

Oliver Cromwell was loved and hated. He was brutal in the campaign against the Irish where no prisoners were taken after his troops stormed the fortress at Drogheda. His treatment of the Irish people was heavy-handed.

Cromwell was a complex figure. He wanted a combination republican-monarchy-parliamentary form of government and ended up as a military ruler. At one point he was accused of being too republican, and at another, of being a traitor to republican principles. In John Bunyan's literary work *Pilgrims Progress*, the character

Mr. Great-heart may have been the allegorical figure of Cromwell. In this book, *Mr. Great-heart* was the protector of pilgrims on their way to the celestial city.

Many people resented Cromwell for his enforcement of the public morality laws, in which theatres were closed and dress codes were enforced. His rule lasted only five years and he died in 1658. His son Richard was not strong enough to maintain power and Charles II returned from France in 1660. Cromwell must be recognized as a military genius, as a man who ended the notion of the *divine right of kings,* and as a man who opened the doors of religious toleration like none before him. He was a saint and a sinner. He was kind and oppressive. Cromwell stands out in English history as a towering military, political, and religious leader.

Levellers and Diggers

The **Levellers** were a 17th century political group in England. They were active during the Civil War and Cromwell's rule. The name came from their belief that all classes of the male population should be allowed to vote (called universal suffrage) and participate in government. The Levellers had widespread support in the Army. Their leader was John Lilburne. He wrote a pamphlet called *The Foundations of Freedom, or an Agreement of the People* which stated three main tenets: **Certain rights of man were unchangeable and beyond the power of government to alter; the authority of government came from the consent of the people; and the powers of government should be separate.** The Levellers believed in the supremacy of Parliament, that it should meet twice a year, and its representatives should be based on population density. They also believed that capital punishment should be abolished for all crimes except murder. Cromwell's regime suppressed them in 1653, and their political influence faded. However, their influence in the long run was significant. Their ideas were part of the American Revolution.

The **Diggers**, sometimes confused with the Levellers, carried their beliefs about equality onto the field of economics. They believed that private land ownership should be abolished. Their name came from an action in 1649 by about forty members who dug up uncultivated common land on St. George's Hill in Surrey, England. They erected tents for dwellings but were soon dispersed by government troops. Their leaders were arrested, tried, and made to pay large fines. The Diggers believed in a form of communism based on the notion that the land was the common treasury of all people. They taught that every able-bodied man should work the soil, and all people should be able to draw from the wealth of that soil according to their needs. One of the leaders of the Diggers, Gerrard Winstanley, opposed organized religion, even though he was a devout Christian. In his work, *The Law of Freedom in a Platform,* he advocated a social/economic system based on communist principles. The Digger movement was also suppressed and faded away in 17th century England. However, its principles were revived in the 19th century (1800s) and were part of the formation of socialist thought in Great Britain and America.

The Restoration

The Puritan Revolution was political but not economic. Property rights were upheld. The more republican minded men of Cromwell's era were not happy with him. They wanted people to have the right to vote even if they did not own property. The Royalists and the Presbyterians despised the *Protectorate* government. Richard Cromwell was not the leader that his father was. The House of Commons made an attempt to restore the glory of Parliament and gain control of the army. They failed.

John Lambert, a man second only to Cromwell in military achievements, was the leader of the army. He got involved behind the scenes to bring back the monarchy. Meanwhile, the army declared itself to be submissive to the new Parliament. Lambert didn't last long. An old Cromwellian general in Scotland took the lead. His name was **George Monk.** He was a soldier of fortune who fought for the Royalists at the beginning of the civil war. After being captured by the Roundheads, he switched sides and fought for Oliver Cromwell. From his post in Scotland, he gained the respect of the Scottish people (unlike Cromwell). He also won the respect of the English republicans.

The situation in London had become very unstable and Monk was asked to come and do something about it. On New Years Day of 1660, with an army of seven thousand, he marched to York where he met with the old Cromwell veteran **Thomas Fairfax.** They rallied a large group of people for a new and free Parliament. Monk then went on to London where he confronted the old Rump Parliament and filled it with new members who were thrown out by Cromwell years earlier. These were mostly Presbyterians who had become Royalists at heart.

The **Restoration** of the Monarchy was now in sight. The new Parliament called upon Charles II (living in exile in France) to return to England. General Monk worked behind the scenes to secure the safety of all who fought against Charles' father in the civil war. A deal was made that retribution would only come to those who actually played a major role in the execution of Charles I.

Charles II

The "Merry Monarch"

A new concept of monarchy began in England. Faith in the doctrine of the *divine right of kings* was dead and Charles II knew it. Parliament, the Common Law, and the Magna Carta would limit his royal authority.

On May 25th, 1660, Charles II returned to England from France. At Dover, General Monk welcomed him with great reverence. The king then went to London in a triumphal procession. The old *Ironsides* soldiers of Cromwell's army lined up to greet him. Presbyterian clergyman presented Charles with a Bible. Whether they were rich or poor, Cavalier or Roundhead, Presbyterian, Anglican, or Independent, these masses were part of a day of celebration not seen in the history of England.

Revenge for the execution of Charles' father was limited. Charles wanted clemency for as many people as possible. Only nine people were executed for treason. The corpses of Cromwell, Ireton (Cromwell's son-in-law), and Bradshaw were yanked out of their coffins at Westminster Abbey and dragged through the streets. Cromwell's son Richard went into exile. The real victor in the Restoration was not actually the king. It was the Parliament. Finally, the king would have to work with it. The army also submitted to it.

Charles II did not prove himself to be an able king. Known as the "Merry Monarch," this king was a notorious womanizer who ruled over the most immoral court in English history. His foreign adventures were indecisive. In 1672, the Treaty of Dover was signed with France, in which the two powers combined their forces against Holland, which was a Protestant country. There was a secret clause in this document. In it, Charles II said he was convinced that the Catholic Faith was the truth, and he would convert to it when the "welfare of his realm permitted it."

Parliament met in 1673 and let Charles know that it was unhappy with the alliance with France and the war against the Dutch. Rumor in England had it that Charles betrayed the nation by taking a bribe from the French monarch, Louis XIV. Anglicans, Puritans, and Presbyterians were alarmed about papal influence and the conversion of James (the Duke of York and the king's brother) to Roman Catholicism. Parliament passed a bill in 1673 called the **Test Act.** It stated that no man could hold office or commission unless he swore *not* to believe in the Catholic doctrine of **transubstantiation.** One of the king's Catholic advisors resigned. James gave up his post of Lord High Admiral because of his Catholic beliefs. James was also in line to become king. Old Cavaliers and Roundheads were now allies in their opposition to Charles.

Another huge development was the marriage of **Mary** (James' daughter by his first marriage) to **William of Orange,** the bright young leader of Holland (he was the grandson of Charles I). William was a strong Protestant and a very able leader who fought off the invasion of Louis XIV of France. This marriage tied two nations together (England and Holland) that had recently been at war with each other. People in England started to look to William as the heir to the English throne.

The Popish Plot

In 1678, a renegade priest named Titus Oates made an accusation that Jesuits and other Catholics were working on a plan to murder the king, bring about a French invasion, massacre Protestants, and set up the Catholic faith as the religion of the British Isles. Many of the members of the House of Lords and the House of Commons believed these accusations. The Duchess of York's private

Secretary was arrested and brought before a magistrate named Sir Edmund Berry Godfrey.

During the time of this examination, Sir Godfrey was found dead one morning at the foot of a place called Primrose Hill. Three men were hanged for the murder, but no one solved any riddle of a conspiracy. Nevertheless, people believed a conspiracy existed. Anglicans and Puritans alike armed themselves for a Catholic confrontation that never happened. The English started a legal mini-reign of terror against Catholics. A large number of Catholic notables went to prison or to the scaffold, with King Charles signing their death warrants against his own desires.

Habeas Corpus

The Earl of Shaftsebury

One of the greatest achievements of this period was the passage of the **Habeas Corpus Act** in 1679. This law was shepherded through the House of Commons by Anthony Ashley Cooper, also known as the **Earl of Shaftesbury.**

The act stated that if a person was arrested, legal grounds for the arrest had to be made public within a few days, or the person was to be released. The king signed on to it. *This right of all Englishmen, whether great or small, could be traced back to the Magna Carta. It became one of the distinguishing characteristics of both English and American constitutional law.*

During the rule of Charles II, the **Whig** and **Tory** parties formed in Parliament. The **Rye House Plot** to take the king's life was a failure. Two leaders of the plot were executed. One was a notable believer in Whig principles. Under Charles, English influence in the Old World diminished, while in the New World it grew. Charles died at age fifty-six. Winston Churchill commented, "Apart from hereditary monarchy, there was not much which Charles believed in this world or another. He wanted to be king, as was his right, and have a pleasant life. He was cynical rather than cruel, and indifferent rather than tolerant." Churchill went on to say that the only significant thing Charles II did was to make sure that the Royal Navy was kept in good shape.

The Second King James

Parliament previously tried to wreck the power of any future Catholic monarch, knowing that James, the former Duke of York was next in line to be king. The Protestants controlled Parliament, and a Privy Council and Protector (**William of Orange**, the Dutch leader and a staunch Protestant) oversaw the royal business. Their plan was that any son who was born to a future Catholic ruler would have to be educated by Protestants. When it didn't work, Parliament tried to exclude the Catholic Duke of York from the throne. Charles decided to dissolve the Parliament. While the reaction against the king's move was strong, it eventually died down. And by the time James II (the Duke of York) came to the throne, no one wanted to go through another civil war over politics or religion.

While the English people did not oppose James' accession to the throne, they were suspicious of his Catholicism. He promised to uphold the rights of Englishmen and support the laws of the land regarding church and state. Nevertheless, the Anglican clergy were uncomfortable with his public practice of the Catholic faith. James proceeded to put Roman Catholics in positions of legal authority. He also gave military commissions to Catholics in violation of the Test Act. One of his relatives led a Protestant rebellion that was brutally suppressed. King James II also built up a large standing army. On November 20, 1681, he dissolved Parliament. At this point, James was clearly attempting to re-establish the Roman Catholic religion. The whole realm was disturbed.

Politics and religion were tied together in England, as they were in other European nations. The English people were deathly afraid of the dominance of a Catholic monarch. The Anglican Church and the Parliament came to realize that James was subverting the faith and Constitution of the land. Some of the king's advisors abandoned him. James continued to put Catholics into the leadership of the army. His army grew into a force as formidable as it was under Cromwell.

In 1688, another civil war seemed inevitable. Both Whigs and old Royalists allied themselves against James. The rebellion spread to the country. The English people feared the loss of their political and religious rights under James. Opposition leaders of the king secretly invited William of Orange, Holland's prince, and husband of the English Mary, to come and save the nation. William agreed to do so at the right time.

James' wife had also given birth to a son. The English were horrified at the prospect of another Catholic in line for the throne. The king saw that events were turning against him. He abandoned his plan to bring Irish regiments to England when word of it got out. Balladeers wrote derisive songs against the Irish and the papists (Roman Catholics). Churchill wrote, "Rumor ran riot. The Irish were coming. The French were coming. The papists were planning a general massacre of the Protestants. The kingdom was (being) sold to Louis XIV of France. Nothing was safe and no one could be trusted. The laws, the Constitution, the Church—all were in jeopardy."

The Glorious Revolution

James tried to backtrack in both politics and religion, but it was too late. On October 19, 1688, William of Orange left the shores of Holland and set sail for England to become its new champion.

His army was composed of Protestant peoples such as the Dutch, Swedes, Danes, Prussians, Scotch, English, and a remnant of French Huguenots. This army numbered about fourteen thousand and came through the Straits of Dover with about five hundred and sixty ships. On November 5, 1688, William landed at Torbay, England. When William was told that it was the anniversary of the Gunpowder Plot, he remarked, "What do you think of Predestination now?"

English people in both town and country were anxiously awaiting the arrival of William of Orange and his wife Mary (the elder daughter of James II). King James' army was quickly deserting to William's side in city after city. James entered into negotiations with the new king, sent his wife and son out of the country, and tried to escape himself. He was captured, but then allowed to escape again. He left English soil and never returned. **The Glorious Revolution** came to England. No blood was shed. William marched his armies into London without firing a shot.

William and Mary

It took about one year to establish the revolution. Parliament passed laws to restrict the monarchy and safeguard the rights of Englishmen. The **Toleration Act** was passed which granted religious liberty to all Christians except Catholics and Unitarians. *The greatest triumph of the new government was the passage of the English Bill of Rights on December 16, 1689. It provided for trial by jury, the right of Englishmen to petition the government for redress of grievances, condemned excessive bail and exorbitant fines, and opposed cruel and unusual punishment. This Bill of Rights also forbade the king to suspend laws, levy taxes, or raise a standing army in peacetime without the consent of Parliament.* William and Mary agreed to these stipulations. The Parliament's triumph over the Monarchy was now complete. William and Mary received their power from the Parliament, and never again would an English monarch defy this body. *The English Bill of Rights became a*

model for future American colonists. Some of its most important elements were put into the American Bill of Rights. William III proved himself to be an able leader. He was an excellent soldier and diplomat. In 1690, he led his troops against a counterrevolution led by James II in Ireland. He defeated their forces at the Battle of Boyne.

However, he was not one of the most popular British monarchs. King William did not quite understand the English or their ways. His skills were used in foreign affairs more than they were in domestic ones. On English soil, it was Parliament that really reformed English government. The House of Commons clearly became the most powerful body, and the English Bill of Rights became possibly the most influential document in promoting the God-given rights of English speaking peoples. During this period, England went through happy and peaceful times.

Excerpts from the 1689 Bill of Rights

This document was the third great charter of English liberty. It was the result of the *Glorious Revolution* of 1688 in which the Crown was given to *William and Mary.* After James II fled England, there was no legal king or Parliament. An extra-legal assembly of magistrates and past members of the House of Commons met on January 22, 1689. They passed an act declaring that they were a true Parliament.

William and Mary were asked to take the throne under the conditions of a *Declaration of Right.* The new Parliament decided to incorporate its principles into an act called the *Bill of Rights.* This legislation eliminated the methods that the first four Stuart kings (James I and II, Charles I and II) used to suppress Parliament.

AN ACT DECLARING THE RIGHTS AND LIBERTIES OF THE SUBJECT AND SETTLING THE SUCCESSION OF THE CROWN.

Whereas the late King James II.....did endeavor to subvert and extirpate the Protestant religion and the laws and liberties of this kingdom by assuming and exercising a power of dispensing and suspending laws, and by executing laws without the consent of Parliament........by violating freedom of election of members to serve in Parliament....and by diverse arbitrary and illegal courses....[the] Parliament is to meet and sit at Westminster....in order to [provide] such an establishment as that their religion, laws, and liberties might not again be in danger of being subverted.....

.....the pretended power [by the king] of suspending laws or executing laws without consent of Parliament is illegal.

.....the commission for erecting the late court of commissioners for ecclesiastical [religious] causes is illegal.

.....it is the right of subjects to petition the king, and all prosecutions [against] such petitioning are illegal.

.....the raising or keeping of a standing army within the kingdom in time of peace, unless it be with consent of Parliament, is against the law.

.....that the subjects which are Protestants may have arms for their defense suitable to their conditions and as allowed by law.

.....election of members of Parliament ought to be free.

.....the freedom of speech and debates or proceedings in Parliament ought not to be impeached or questioned in any court or place out[side] of Parliament.

.....excessive bail ought not to be required, nor excessive fines imposed, nor cruel and unusual punishments inflicted.

.....jurors ought to be duly impaneled and returned.

.....promises of fines and forfeitures of particular persons before conviction are illegal and void.

.....for redress of all grievances and for the amending, strengthening, and preserving of laws, parliaments ought to be held frequently.

This Bill of Rights acknowledged the providence and merciful goodness of God to the British nation. It established an oath of office for public officials. It stated who the heirs to the English throne should be. *The 1689 Bill of Rights was not the product of revolutionaries, it was written by those who were part of a counter-revolution. This bill did not establish new rights. It simply sought by law to establish and uphold the rights of English people that were already in existence.*

Glossary

Anglican Church—The established (state) Church of England. It has an Episcopal church government (a group of bishops). The Archbishop of Canterbury is the highest bishop and the king or queen is the head. In the more modern Anglican Communion of churches, most of the congregations are not state churches.

Archbishop of Canterbury—The head bishop of the Church of England. His seat is in the small city of Canterbury, in Southeast England.

Burgher—A middle-class townsman or borough dweller.

Commonwealth—From 1649 to 1660, this term was used to describe the English nation in which Cromwell and the Parliament protected the common interests of the people. Generally, the term is usually applied to a nation or state in which the common good of the people is carried out politically in a representative government such as a republic or democracy.

Common Law—The law in England that was established through custom and the decisions of the courts and magistrates. This was a part of law that was separate from laws passed by legislation.

Dissenters—Protestants who refused to accept the doctrines and worship methods of the Established (Anglican) Church of England.

Divine Right of Kings—The belief that kings (or queens) were ordained of God to rule people.

Elizabethan Compromise—The approach that Queen Elizabeth took toward the Church of England in which the Church was officially Protestant but kept some of the forms of worship from the Roman Catholic Church. In doctrine, it was more Protestant than Catholic, but the Puritans believed it did not go far enough in separating itself from the Roman Church.

Franchise—The right to vote in elections for public office.

Gentry—A landowning class of people that was ranked just below the nobility.

High Church Anglicanism—The practice of some Anglicans in which seven sacraments and the Mass were conducted with similarities to the Roman Catholic Church. A greater emphasis was placed on a sacramental life than on individual conversion and lifestyle. *Low Church Anglicanism* had only two sacraments (Baptism and Communion) and had more similarities to Protestantism.

Judicial Review—A system of justice where laws passed by Parliament or Congress can be reviewed by a court to test whether they conform to the common law (England) or the Constitution (United States).

Long Parliament—The legislative body of England that met from 1640 to 1653 without a break. It fought for civil and religious liberties against King Charles I and declared England to be a Commonwealth after he was executed. Cromwell dissolved what was left of it (the Rump Parliament) in 1653.

Monopoly—In older English times, this was a privilege granted by a king to a business for the right to sell a product in a given area without competition.

Presbyterians—A religious body that followed the teachings of John Calvin. They were strong believers in predestination. Presbyterians believed in a church government composed of elders who ruled local churches and a larger *presbytery* that made decisions pertaining to the whole denomination. Some of them were Puritans. They were very active politically in England during the 1600s, and almost took control of the government during the period of the English Civil War.

Protestants—A large and diverse group of Trinitarian Christians that were not part of the Roman Catholic Church. They were initially composed of Calvinists (Reformed), Lutherans, Anglicans, and Anabaptists. They grew into a wide variety of churches and denominations and emphasized a return to simpler church worship, believed that the scriptures were the final authority for the faith, and taught that salvation was by the grace of God and not human merit.

Rump Parliament—The part of Parliament that remained after Oliver Cromwell threw out the Presbyterians and others in 1648. Cromwell then disbanded this remnant of a legislative body in 1653.

Separatist—A group within the Puritans that favored total separation from the Church of England on the grounds that the Church had too much of the flavor of Roman Catholicism in it. They formed independent churches. The American *Pilgrims* were separatists.

Stuart—The family of the kings of England from 1603–1714, except during the period of the Commonwealth and Cromwell's rule.

Squire—An English country gentleman who owned land.

Tory—In 1679-80, a person who wanted to keep James, Duke of York in line to become king of England, even though he was Roman Catholic. Later, a Tory was a member of a political party in England opposed to the Whig party.

Transubstantiation—The Roman Catholic Church doctrine that the bread and wine of the Eucharist are changed, during the Mass, into the actual body and blood of Christ.

Whig—Member of a political party in England in the 17th, 18th, and 19th centuries that promoted reform and the rights of Parliament.

NEW ENGLAND

In 1620, a group called the **Pilgrims** landed at Plymouth Rock on the shore of Cape Cod Bay in Massachusetts. The Pilgrims were the *Separatist* wing of the Puritans, and they were sometimes called **Brownists** after one of their early leaders, Robert Brown. They preferred to separate themselves from the Church of England completely, while other Puritans tried to reform the church from within.

In the early 1600s, English authorities decided to persecute and imprison the Separatist congregations set up in London and some other areas. At a small town in northern England called **Scrooby,** the Pilgrims wrote a church covenant in 1606. In it, they affirmed themselves as a self-governing body. This congregation was blessed with the leadership of **William Brewster, John Robinson**, and **William Bradford.** In 1608, the congregation at Scrooby fled to Holland. Members from other separatist English congregations joined them.

They formed a religious body at Amsterdam and later moved to Leiden. While the Pilgrims were in Holland, they established a fruitful congregation and were free to worship as they pleased. After eleven or twelve years in Holland, William Bradford wrote about the problems of old age setting in among them, and the lack of emigrants (people moving to Holland) from England. He was also concerned that some of their children were in danger of youthful immorality, "the manifold temptations of the place, and were (being) drawn away by evil examples into extravagant and dangerous courses." The Pilgrims also had a desire to advance the gospel of Christ to the remote parts of the world. America, with its wilderness and unconverted natives, was the place for them to go.

Pilgrims on the Mayflower

After getting their financial support in London, the Separatists returned to England in a small craft called the *Speedwell.* Some additional Pilgrims and a few other enterprising Englishmen joined their ranks. The group left England with two ships, the *Speedwell* and the larger *Mayflower.* The *Speedwell* was not seaworthy and the voyagers had to return to England. Finally, the *Mayflower* set sail alone from Plymouth, England in September 1620, with 102 men, women, and children. This mixed company of "saints" and "strangers" endured a rough Atlantic passage of 65 days.

The Mayflower Compact

Upon arrival, 41 men signed the Mayflower Compact, agreeing to form a government and make laws for the colony at Plymouth. They elected **John Carver** as their first governor. Below are the words of the *Compact.*

In the name of God, amen. We whose names are underwritten, the loyal subjects of our dread sovereign Lord King James, by the grace of God, the king and defender of the faith of Great Britain, France, and Ireland. Having undertaken, for the glory of God, and the advancement of the Christian faith and honor of our king and country, a voyage to plant the first colony in the northern parts of Virginia, do by those present solemnly and mutually in the presence of God, and of one another, covenant and combine ourselves together into a civil body politic; for our better ordering, and preservation and furtherance of the ends aforesaid; and by virtue hereof to enact, constitute, and frame such just and equal laws, ordinances, acts, constitutions, and offices from time to time, as shall be thought most fit and convenient for the general good of the colony: unto which we promise all due submission and obedience. In witness whereof we have here subscribed our names at Cape Cod, November 11, in the year of the reign of our Sovereign Lord King James of England, France, and Ireland the eighteenth, and of Scotland the fifty-fourth, and in the year of our Lord, 1620.

The Pilgrims expected to settle within the territorial limits of their Virginia Company charter. But adverse winds and shoals forced them to turn north and anchor the *Mayflower* inside the tip of Cape Cod, Massachusetts. They made this compact while they were still in the harbor getting ready for their landing and exploration of the coast. The settlement was named Plymouth. The Pilgrims decided to write the *Mayflower Compact* because some of the "strangers" among them were making discontented speeches. They were also uncertain of their legal status since they ended up north of their charter granted by King James.

The Mayflower Compact became a milestone in the concept of co-operative government under God. It established in the New World the notion that free men would bind themselves together for the common good, respect each other's rights, and make laws that all agreed to obey. Governor William Bradford wrote a wonderful account of the Pilgrims' journey and settlement in the book called *Of Plymouth Plantation.*

Massachusetts Bay
The American Israel of the Puritans

Ten years after the Plymouth settlement of the Pilgrims, about 1000 Puritans on eighteen ships set sail for the new world. In 1630 they landed in the Massachusetts Bay area and formed their colony with **John Winthrop** serving as Governor. Envisioning themselves as the "new Israel" on the American continent, these hardy people quickly formed a strong society in New England.

Their first winter, like the Pilgrim's experience before them, was a struggle. They persevered however, and tamed the wilderness they believed the Lord had given them.

Some of the Puritans who came to America had previously experienced **Archbishop Laud's** jails and tortures back in England. To avoid the continual harassment of Laud, men like **Thomas Hooker, Charles Chauncey, John Cotton,** and **John Davenport** came to Massachusetts Bay. This Puritan colony had some of the best-trained theological minds of the day.

The Puritans came for religious freedom to be sure. But they did not intend to open the doors of **liberty of conscience** in matters of religion. While this group of Puritans was not Separatist, their version of the Church of England in the American wilderness ended up as **Congregationalism.** They also believed the civil magistrates had the responsibility to suppress false doctrine, and they restricted voting to those who were members of approved churches.

The Puritans had the ideal of the *Holy Commonwealth*. This ideal involved the consecration of church, state, business, and education according to the Word of God. During the first generation of Puritanism on American shores, anyone who did not attend religious services was brought before a magistrate and fined. Those who charged excessive prices for goods were also fined. Many of the laws of the Old Testament were enforced. The Puritans established Christian public education in Boston. They believed that one of ways to defeat "the old deluder Satan" was to educate children so that they could read and understand the Bible.

Divisions and persecutions also developed in the colony. Thomas Hooker, pastor of the congregation at Newtown (now Cambridge), left for Connecticut after disagreement with the spiritual leaders in Massachusetts Bay. In January of 1639, the *Fundamental Orders of Connecticut* was adopted as the territory's constitution.

The most famous of the dissidents in Massachusetts was **Roger Williams.** After serving as a pastor in both Plymouth and Salem, his ideas about liberty of conscience brought him into conflict with the leaders of the bay area **theocracy.** Williams also said that the colonists had no right to take land from the Native

Americans even if they had a royal charter. He was tried for heretical ideas and banished from the colony. He then fled to Rhode Island where he founded the town of **Providence** in 1636. Williams strongly believed that the civil government should have no power over a person's right to worship God according to their conscience. Williams also denied that religious conformity was necessary for social stability. After he arrived at Rhode Island in the dead of winter, the Indians of the area helped him to survive.

Anne Hutchinson was also a famous dissenter. She followed John Cotton to America. Soon thereafter, she set up a discussion center at her home in Boston where she invited others to come and analyze the sermons of the town's ministers. She ultimately came to the conclusion that the theocratic ideal of the Puritans emphasized the letter of the law and not the spirit. A large portion of the townspeople sided with her. A session of the General Court was convened and Hutchinson was brought to trial. Claiming that she learned through "immediate revelation," the court disagreed and banished her. Her brother-in-law, Reverend John Wheelwright, was also banished as one of her followers.

The Puritan leaders jailed and fined a few Presbyterian dissenters in 1646 and 1647. Four Quakers were executed in 1659, and a few Baptists were beaten and fined for conducting unauthorized religious services in a house.

While John Winthrop and most Puritans favored theocratic **oligarchy**, other Puritans wanted a more popular or representative government (including Hooker and Williams). One of the results of this tension was the writing of the **Massachusetts Body of Liberties** in 1641. Winthrop conceded that the framers of it were acting "to frame a body of grounds of laws *in resemblance to a Magna Carta.*" This very detailed document provided for the liberties of men, women, children, servants, aliens, and "dumb animals," and recognized that individual liberty depended upon the right to appeal to the courts as a last resort. It guaranteed the right of a trial by jury and the right to have counsel (a lawyer). This colonial set of laws guaranteed freedom of speech and petition at public meetings. The state was also prohibited from taking property without fair compensation to the owners. *This Body of Liberties became one of the models for the Bill of Rights that was later to become part of the U.S. Constitution.*

Excerpts from the Massachusetts Body of Liberties, 1641

1. No man's life shall be taken away, no man's honor or good name stained, no man shall be arrested....nor in any way punished, no man shall be deprived of his wife or children, nor shall his goods be taken from him....except it be by some express law of the country....established by a general court and sufficiently published, or in case of the

defect of a law in any particular case, by the Word of God.

2. Every person within this jurisdiction, whether inhabitant or for-
   eigner, shall enjoy the same justice and law....which we constitute
   and execute towards one another without partiality or delay.

5. No man shall be compelled to do any public work or service unless
   it be grounded upon some act of the general Court....

8. No man's cattle or goods shall be taken for any public use unless it
   be by warrant grounded upon some act of the general Court, nor
   [can they be taken] without such reasonable prices as the ordinary
   rates of the country do afford.

12. Every man...free or not free shall have the liberty to come to any
    public Court, Council, or Town Meeting, and either by speech or
    writing, make any....question, or present any necessary motion,
    complaint, petition, bill, or information....

22. No man in any suit or action against another shall falsely pretend
    great debts or damages to vex his adversary. If it appears that he
    has done so, the Court shall have power to set a reasonable fine on
    his head.

26. Every man that finds himself unfit to plead his own cause in any
    Court shall have the liberty to employ any man....to help him.
    Provided that he give him no fee for his pains. This shall not
    exempt the person from answering such questions as the court
    thinks fit to demand of him.

30. It shall be the liberty of both plaintiff and defendant, and every
    delinquent, to challenge any of the Jurors....

36. It shall be in the liberty of every man who is sentenced or con-
    demned in any inferior court, to make their appeal to the Court of
    Assistants....and every man shall have liberty to complain to the
    General Court of any injustice that is done to him in any Court of
    Assistants or other.

41. No man shall be twice sentenced by Civil Justice for one and the same crime, offense, or trespass.

47. No man shall be put to death without the testimony of two or three witnesses or that which is equivalent.

48. Every inhabitant of the country shall have the free liberty to search and view any rules, records, or registers of any Court or office....

60. No church censure shall degrade or take away from any man, any Civil Dignity, Office, or Authority he shall have in the Commonwealth.

70. All freeman called to give advice, vote, verdict, or sentence in any Court...shall have the freedom to do it according to their true judgments and consciences....

79. If any man does not leave his wife a competent portion of his estate [at his death], she shall be relieved upon a just complaint to the General Court.

85. If any servant shall flee from the tyranny and cruelty of their master to the house of any freeman of the same town, they shall be protected and sustained there until due [court] order be taken for their relief....

92. No man shall exercise any tyranny or cruelty toward any brute creatures [animals] which are usually kept for man's use.

94. *[This section listed all of the crimes for which a person could be executed (capital crimes). They were taken from the Old Testament books of Exodus, Numbers, Leviticus, and Deuteronomy. The crimes were murder, idolatry, blasphemy, witchcraft, homosexuality, bestiality, adultery, kidnapping, and false testimony that could cost another person their life].*

ENLIGHTENMENT AND AWAKENING

By the end of the 1600s, England became the land of **John Locke** and **Isaac Newton.** It was a land of coffeehouses and newspapers. It was a land of scientific discovery and political theory. It was a land that had experienced political revolution, religious upheaval, plague, and hard won human liberties. The greatest political philosopher of this period was John Locke.

John Locke

His writings were varied. He wrote *Reasonableness of Christianity, Letters Concerning Toleration, Essay Concerning Human Understanding, First Treatise on Government,* and many other works. Locke believed in both divine revelation as given in Holy Scripture, and Natural Law, which was based upon man's innate moral sense. His writings were influential in the thinking of Thomas Jefferson and others in the American colonies. While not necessarily an original thinker, Locke clearly put forth ideas on government that were built on the best political theories in the Western Christian world. While some have concluded that he was a **Deist** and not a Christian, Locke based his beliefs on the notion of a sovereign God who gave gifts and laws to men, and had an absolute right to judge them with rewards and punishments in the next life. John Locke continued to build upon the English legal tradition that there were certain inalienable rights given to men by God that government could not take away. During the late 17th century, Locke wrote his major political work *The Second Treatise on Civil Government.* In it, he emphasized the idea of the existence of a contract between rulers and those who were ruled. Locke's view also promoted the idea that it was the responsibility of government to protect property and the liberty of propertied men. Locke's philosophy may have come partially from the **Levellers** (see page 32). It is safe to say that John Locke's **Social Contract Theory** led to limited and constitutional government.

England entered into a period of peace, renewed culture, and prosperity under the reign of **Queen Anne.** The violent political and religious struggles were over. Debate over ideas did not mean violent action, and England settled into the fruits of **The Enlightenment.** *Those who followed enlightenment ideas believed that human reason could overcome the evils that existed in church, state, and society. They*

52

believed that human rights could be advanced in the world by the rational application of knowledge. Sometimes these ideas were secular and sometimes they were mixed with Christianity. The Enlightenment played a significant role in bringing down the arbitrary power of government and helping men realize that they possessed rights and property that could not be abused by those in power.

Samuel Rutherford, a Scottish Presbyterian theologian, was also an important figure because of his writing of the book *Lex Rex* (The Law and the Prince) in 1644. This book was written to refute the writings of John Maxwell, an Anglican clergyman, who was defending the notion of the divine right of kings. Rutherford argued that the authority of government rested on two foundations, divine law and the law of nature, and both were to bind the king. Rutherford published his work while he was in London helping to write the **Westminster Confession.**

Meanwhile, in the thirteen colonies of America, progress was taking place on most fronts. Population doubled each generation. The ability to attain middle class status was much easier in America than in Europe. Boston and Philadelphia became prosperous. But the original New England Puritanism was in decline and the Quakers in Pennsylvania had become less religious as they became prosperous. Town records show that although they were only one-seventh of the population of Philadelphia, the Quakers made up half the town's population that paid over 100 pounds in taxes.

If religious zeal was fading away, there was a movement to revive and restore zealous Christian behavior and character. Known as **The Great Awakening,** this event (or series of events) proved to be very significant in terms of religion, culture, and politics. It probably started in 1719 in the Raritan Valley of New York when Theodore Frelinghuysen, a German pastor of a Dutch Reformed Church led a series of meetings. The movement did not begin in cities such as Boston, New York, or Philadelphia, but in the country. The chief emphasis was on what is called **Pietism.** This is a Christian philosophy that encourages a quiet and holy life, and emphasizes personal morality rather than doctrinal creeds. A frontier movement at first, this religious awakening was led by preachers who wanted people to hear the message, live the message, and read the Word of God for themselves.

Jonathon Edwards

News of this movement spread north and was picked up by a minister at a Northampton, Massachusetts church named **Jonathan Edwards.** Edwards was one of the most gifted thinkers in America at the time. From Puritan ancestors, Edwards entered Yale slightly before his thirteenth birthday. He graduated first in his class and wrote speculative papers on such things as the Mind, Spiders, the Theory of Atoms, and the Nature of Being. Edwards took over the church at Northampton when his grandfather, the previous pastor, died. Edwards' most famous sermon, *Sinners in the Hands of an Angry God* (1741), caused some in his congregation to shriek and cry out for mercy. The message was published and read all over the colonies. Edwards also emphasized more than just hell and damnation. He emphasized the bounty of God's goodness and the need for people to look to this goodness with joy. Edwards wrote a discourse called *God Glorified in the Work of Redemption,* which insisted that human beings should find happiness in the excellence and beauty of God. Edwards stated that persons of lesser learning and smaller mental capacities could enjoy God just as much as those that possessed greater learning. This added to the democratic spirit that was growing in the colonies. Edwards promoted a religion that was accepted by people of a wide variety of creedal backgrounds and ethnic origins. His energizing of a new frontier religion enabled Americans and newly arrived immigrants to understand that personal conversion to Christ, leading useful and good lives, and having a love for God and fellow man were the main ingredients necessary for them to walk in the way of salvation.

Edwards was the man who crystallized the Great Awakening, but **George Whitefield** (1714-1770) was the man who made it spread like wildfire. Whitefield was a speaker with spectacular gifts. Known as the Great Itinerant, he preached the Christian message with clarity and power. Unlike his English counterpart, **John Wesley,** Whitefield did not concern himself with organizing societies (e.g. Wesley's Methodists) but simply preached from town to town throughout the American colonies. He appealed to all religious denominations. While the established churches in Calvinist Boston shunned him, his preaching in that town met with great success. He made seven continental tours of America between 1740 and 1770. Others helped to spread the message of a purer commitment to Christ such as William Tennent (1673-1745) and John Davenport (1716-1757). Samuel Davies (1723-1761) also spread the Christian message throughout the Mid-Atlantic States (especially Virginia) at the tail end of this religious expansion. Probably the most influential minister of the period stayed in England. John Wesley's accomplishments in preaching and in forming the Methodist religious societies have been unequalled even to this day. Wesley opposed the American Revolution.

While this awakening had a profound influence spiritually, it was also a movement that inspired some to a more rational view of life. Unitarianism also started to gain ground in New England, partially as a result of the Awakening.

The Great Awakening Americanized the Protestant religion. Individual experience in conversion, moral fervor, downgrading the clergy, and reducing liturgical emphasis were the results of this movement. *It was also an important pre-revolution event. The difference between the American and French Revolutions was that the French conflict was anti-religious and the American uprising was pro-religious. Culturally, The Great Awakening combined religious experience and ethics with some of the ideas of the Enlightenment. It played a role in helping Americans appreciate their historic rights under the rule of English law.*

Glossary

Deist—A person who believes in God on purely rational grounds without relying on divine revelation as found in the scriptures, the church, or the realm of the spirit. A deist also believes that God created the universe and its natural laws, but does not play an active role in its current operation.

Enlightenment—A philosophical movement in 18th century Europe that emphasized learning and rational thought. A great emphasis was placed on being skeptical toward established religion, politics, and society.

Social Contract Theory—The political theory that individuals unite themselves for various reasons, give up some of their rights as individuals, and form a governing body to issue laws for the good of the whole group or society.

Westminster Confession—A document produced by an assembly of Presbyterian ministers at Westminster Abbey in London, during the years 1643-1648. The teachings in it cover such things as the sacred scriptures, salvation, the sacraments, the Trinity, the Church, the civil authorities, and the Last Judgment.

BOSTON—TOWN OF RADICALS

While the religious zeal of the Puritans was fading, Massachusetts moved into the 18th century with strong social, political, and religious structures. The hallmarks of Bostonians were hard work, an orderly society, and an educated population.

Boston was a prime example of a bubbling new world city. It was full of shop-keepers, silversmiths, seaman, blacksmiths, brewers, soap boilers, and importers. Religion and law were important to this solid mix of poor, middle class, and wealthy citizens. But a small criminal element dwelt there too.

By the 1760s, these New Englanders fully appreciated their rights as English citizens. Many fought for their mother country in the **French and Indian War.** The English way of life and the Protestant religion had been preserved in America. Some Bostonians were prone to rioting in order to uphold these rights.

A smallpox plague hit the town in 1764. Unlike the plague forty-one years ear-lier, the town's leaders (called **selectmen**) supported a major inoculation. Their decision was justified. This treatment, which was advocated by Cotton Mather years earlier, was given to 4977 people. Only 46 of them died. Those who got smallpox the "natural way" totaled 699 people. Of this group, 124 died. John Adams was inoculated during this epidemic. Boston also suffered from a major economic downturn in 1765, and the city had a high mortality rate for women in childbirth. Hardship and death were part of the life of New England society.

This was the town of the **Sons of Liberty**, a semi-secret group of men who rabble roused in opposition to the English colonial government that they thought was disregarding their rights. Some would call them a mob that disregarded the rights of those who opposed them. Lacking a single leader for a while, **Samuel Adams** became their champion at the right moment. This failed businessman (he was a brewer) was a master at politics. Strangely enough, he was also Boston's tax collector for a short time. His leniency in collections was well known, and at one point, he was in danger of going to jail for lack of collections until **John Hancock** got him off the hook.

Sam Adams worked behind the scenes, always moving and shaking, always weighing things until the right situations arrived for his skills. John Hancock was an extremely wealthy man who was noted for a lavish lifestyle. He was also noted for his philanthropy. His business enterprises employed a large percentage of

Boston's population. Hancock's parties and extravaganzas for the common people of Boston made him very popular.

In 1765, the **Stamp Act** was passed. This act required every legal document, newspaper, or commercial paper to have a stamp affixed to it. It was applied to all the thirteen colonies and all classes of people. The cost would vary according to the document. England needed tax money to maintain its rule in the colonies. The lawyers, with tons of legal papers, would be the hardest hit.

British Prime Minister George Grenville thought the tax would be fair. However, the response from the colonies was negative. While Virginia made its opposition known through men like the eloquent Patrick Henry, Boston voiced its opposition to the act through some rioting. The **Liberty Tree** made its debut in 1765. Effigies (stuffed figures) of British officials were hanged and burned. On August 14, English Lieutenant Governor Thomas Hutchinson ordered the sheriff to take down the effigies. After looking over the crowds, the sheriff decided not to. The *Sons of Liberty* were on the march. These unruly crowds intimidated people who were on the side of the British government. They also destroyed some property, although no lives were lost and few people were hurt. Parliament was faced with a general defiance by the colonists and repealed the Stamp Act in 1766.

The **Quartering Act** also went through Parliament at Grenville's prodding. It required Americans to provide living quarters, fuel, candles, transportation, cider, and beer for British troops stationed in the colonies. The colonists detested this Act.

In 1767, another crisis occurred. Chancellor of the Exchequer (the Treasury department) Charles Townshend persuaded Parliament to place import taxes on all tea, lead, paper, and paint that were brought into the colonies. These were called the **Townshend Acts.** Townshend assumed that since the colonists bitterly opposed an internal tax such as the one on stamps, they would not have major objections to external taxes collected at their ports. He was wrong. The colonists began a boycott of British goods and Parliament repealed the Townshend Acts in 1770, *except for the tax on tea.*

The British fired up their presence in Boston over the next few years and the oven was getting hot. British soldiers and some of Boston's inhabitants had been sparring for some time. Troops had been quartered (taken residence) in citizen's homes against their wills. A threatening atmosphere developed. On the moonlit evening of Monday March 5, 1770, things boiled over. At about eight o'clock, a young boy was beaten by a soldier. One thing led to another. A confrontation took place between a crowd of townspeople and a British soldier named Montgomery. He called for help. Eight other British regulars arrived. A Captain Preston, who had a good reputation among the colonists, was their commander.

He ordered his soldiers to load and prime their muskets, but he put himself between them and the people as a buffer. **Henry Knox** (the plump and likeable bookstore owner who was later to become chief of artillery for George Washington's army) begged Preston to take his men away. It did not happen. **Crispus Attucks,** a man well over six feet tall, attacked Preston but ended up hitting Montgomery with a club. He was fired upon and took two bullets to the chest. He and four others were killed. This was the **Boston Massacre.** Captain Preston and his men were arrested the next morning for murder. **John Adams** and **Josiah Quincy** defended the British soldiers in criminal court. The mob's violence that March evening did not sit well with either man. To their great honor, they were interested in justice. The soldiers received a fair trial and were all acquitted of murder. The jury's foreman was even a Son of Liberty. Two soldiers were, however, convicted of manslaughter and branded on their hands. However, the people of Boston did not forget this "massacre," even though the soldiers were lawfully acquitted. It became added fuel for the revolutionary fire that was burning in the heart of many a Bostonian.

In 1772, the Boston Town Committee wrote up a **Violation of Rights** that the British Government committed against their colony. In this same year, British Governor Thomas Hutchinson announced that his salary and the salaries of the judges would be paid by the English Crown and not by the colonists. The Massachusetts leaders bitterly opposed this because they believed that it would make these officials free from their local control. After a town meeting in which Governor Hutchinson said that it was none of the town's business who paid him, Sam Adams moved that a committee be appointed "to state the rights of the colonists....as men, as Christians, and as subjects; and to communicate this to the several towns in this Province, and to the World."

The Violation of Rights declared that the colonists had the right to life, liberty, and property. It also declared that the colonists had the right to practice the Christian religion according to the dictates of their consciences. The writers of this document stated that their rights as Christians could be best understood by reading the New Testament and studying the teachings of Jesus Christ. They appealed to the Magna Carta as proof of their rights and stated that King John was pressured with the threat of the sword to grant the barons their rights, as they might have to do to rescue those rights from British tyranny. Sam Adams and his Sons of Liberty also said clearly that the people born in the American colonies possessed the rights of all Englishmen and were entitled to all liberties and privileges of subjects born in Great Britain.

The *Violation of Rights* promoted an independent judiciary and stated, "There shall be one rule of justice for rich and poor...." and made it clear that government was not to take men's property without their consent. Twelve items were listed in which the British government violated the rights of Bostonians. The first item said the most when it complained that the British Parliament assumed "power of legislation for the Colonists in all cases whatsoever, without obtaining the consent of the inhabitants...."

In 1773, Parliament passed the **Tea Act.** The British government was disturbed over the impending financial collapse of the **East India Company.** Seven years supply of tea laid in storage along the Thames River in London. To help this company avoid bankruptcy, the government decided to give it a monopoly in the American market. The colonists had been smuggling in Dutch tea at cheaper prices than the English offered. However, with the passage of the Tea Act, the East India Company would pay this tax in England and the colonists would never see it. The tea would also be sold for less than the smuggled Dutch tea. This would seem to be a good deal for the Americans, but it didn't fly. Many colonists thought that if England could establish a monopoly on tea, what products would be next? The British government also set up consignees in the colonies to act as local distributors who would make all the profits. The local retail shopkeepers who were cut out of the deal resented this. In Boston, Governor Hutchinson set up his own clique to get the rights to sell the tea.

The negative reaction in the colonies was quick. Radical and conservative elements came together to oppose the Tea Act. The English ships laden with tea were expected in November. Mass meetings were proclaimed and the Sons of Liberty went on the march again. British redcoats on Castle Island and Ships of War in the harbor sat waiting for the tea to arrive. On November 28, the *Dartmouth* arrived with the first load of tea. The next morning, Boston was posted with this historic proclamation:

Friends! Brethren! Countrymen! That worst of plagues, the detested tea shipped for this port by the East India Company, is now arrived in the Harbour; the hour of destruction, or manly opposition to the machanitions of Tyranny, stares you in the face; every friend to his country, to Himself, and to Posterity, is now called upon to meet at Faneuil Hall, at nine o'clock this day, at which time the bells will ring to make united and successful resistance to this last, worst, and most destructive measure of Administration. Boston. Nov. 29, 1773.

It was in this political climate that Paul Revere became a legend. Two more British ships, the *Beaver* and the *Eleanor* came to port at Griffith's Wharf. Mass meetings continued. Sam Adams' people came out in full force. The Masons met. Paul Revere's two clubs, the North Caucus and Saint Andrew's Lodge met. Inflammatory speeches were underway. On December 16, 1773, a band of colonists (including Revere) headed out for the British tea ships in the harbor under cover of darkness. Over one hundred men loosely disguised as Indians boarded the three ships and broke open the tea chests and dumped their contents into the water. This was the **Boston Tea Party.** British Admiral Montague, who was staying in town that night, watched the episode from a distance. The men who did it were not uncontrolled rabble. They were cool and sensible.

The Committee of Correspondence wrote up an account of what happened that same day. Paul Revere, an excellent horseman as well as silversmith, was chosen to be the courier of the letter and take it to Philadelphia and New York. He made the round trip back to Boston in eleven days, covering about sixty miles a day by horse, not an easy job by anyone's standards.

Radical Whigs and Sons of Liberty in both New York and Philadelphia supported Boston's destruction of the tea. John Adams spoke favorably of the Tea Party while Benjamin Franklin, in London at the time, thought it was a lawless act that had to be paid for by the Bostonians in the amount of eighteen thousand pounds.

The English government retaliated by passing the **Intolerable Acts** in 1774. Increased military presence was set up in Boston and the port was closed until the city agreed to pay for the tea that was destroyed. General Thomas Gage was sent to town and became the acting governor of Massachusetts. Gage was well known and liked. He was cautious and peaceable by nature. He also fought alongside colonists in the French and Indian War, and had an American wife. Bostonians had high hopes for his sense of fair play. He was, however, sent to shut down Boston harbor, and he did it with efficiency. With soldiers, marines, and ships at his command, the British General intended to beat Boston into submission. Tensions grew rapidly as colonists and militias started to store ammunition. General Gage's troops were being increased (and somewhat decreased by desertions). In the winter of 1775, Paul Revere and others kept night watch on the movements of the British. In the spring of 1775, Gage was aware that the English government was getting impatient with his inaction. He also knew that the colonists outside of Boston were storing gunpowder and arms. King George commanded that these stores be seized.

Spies were moving around on both sides. Governor Gage had hoped to see the rebellion cool down, but it got hotter. He therefore decided to move against the rebel's store of arms at Concord. Sam Adams and John Hancock left Boston and were thought to be somewhere near Lexington. Gage may have wanted to arrest them. British troops were starting preparations and word got out among the citizens that something was about to happen. On Sunday the sixteenth of April, Paul Revere rode out to Lexington to warn Adams and Hancock. He then returned to Boston.

Meanwhile, Gage was preparing to march to Concord and destroy the rebel's weapons. The Bostonians watched. It was agreed that they were to be warned by the lanterns in Christ's Church if the British soldiers decided to move, whether by land or sea. The British moved on Concord. The lanterns shined in the church steeple, and Paul Revere (and the less famous Billy Dawes) rode out to warn the countryside of the coming British attack. He also rode into history, poetry, and legendry. The war had begun.

It was a war with mixed interests. Those interests were economic, political, and religious. *What has to be remembered is that the purpose of the war was to restore American's rights, and those rights had a history going back through 17th century England to the Magna Carta itself in 1215 A.D. In this sense, it was really a counter-revolution designed to reclaim what had been lost to the British Crown and Parliament. The colonists decided to do battle with mother England in order to preserve their historic English rights.*

The Sons of Liberty

This group of men was a semi-secret society that had oaths and a secret language. It originated in Boston and developed in the other American colonies. It was organized to oppose the Stamp Act. Some of the leaders of the *Sons of Liberty* were Samuel Adams, John Hancock, Paul Revere, and Oliver Wendell. In this society there were probably two elements; the more public and respectable element, and the element that came out to intimidate people and do property damage. In some cases, the intimidating mobs of the *Sons* were more powerful than the law itself in Boston. They had a hand in the Boston Massacre, the opposition to the Stamp Act, the tarring and feathering of British revenue agents, and the Boston Tea Party. They promoted the *Liberty Tree* and hung the effigies of English officials and their colonial supporters. These men effectively used the printing press to promote their cause. Their not-so-secret meetings in the night were gatherings for debate and planning sessions for action. Numerous local chapters of the *Sons of Liberty* formed the **Committees of Correspondence** to inspire resistance to British political and economic actions. The *Sons* also helped to enforce the policy of **non-importation,** in which American merchants refused to import goods that were carried to the colonies on British ships.

Brief Biography

Samuel Adams

- September 16, 1722—Born in Boston's South End. His father was Samuel Adams Sr. (known as *Deacon* Adams, a pillar in the Congregational Church), who was a merchant and brewer. Samuel Jr. was also the cousin of John Adams.

- 1740—Samuel Adams attends Harvard College. His parents hope that he will enter the ministry. He attends this school during the time of the Great Awakening. In his senior year, he is fined five shillings for drinking rum on campus.

- After leaving Harvard, Adams starts out as a business apprentice. He is let go after a short period of time. He later lends 1000 pounds to a friend who quickly loses it and does not repay him. He also fails in running his father's brewery.

- 1746—At age 24, Adams is elected one of the clerks in the Boston Market.

- By 1748, the Great Awakening fades, as do the hopes for a Puritan renewal in Boston. Samuel Adams opposes the commercial and moneymaking spirit of the town. He believes it leads to weakened morality and the destruction of the people's love of liberty.

- 1748—Sam and some friends organize a secret club and publish a newspaper called the *Independent Advertiser*. His writings oppose some of the British colonial laws.

- 1753—Sam Adams is elected Town Scavenger.

- 1756—Adams is elected Boston's Tax Collector

- 1757—His wife dies. He is left with two children.

- 1764—Fearing that the British government would use the tax on molasses for a Royal military presence in the colonies, Sam Adams opposes the *Sugar Act* of Parliament.

- 1765—The *Stamp Act* is passed in Parliament. Adams vigorously opposes it. It is repealed the next year.

- 1767—The *Townshend Acts* are passed. Adams opposes these taxes on the colonies also. These taxes are all repealed in 1770, except the tax on tea.

- March 5, 1770—The Boston Massacre takes place.

- 1772—Spurred on by Adams, Boston's leaders set up a *Committee of Correspondence*.

- December 16, 1773—Sam Adams leads the Boston resistance to the monopoly given to the *East India Company* to sell tea in the colonies. A group of colonists dump tea into the Boston harbor from British ships. This act is known as the *Boston Tea Party*.

- 1774—The British Parliament responds with passage of the *Intolerable Acts*. Boston's port is closed and town meetings are restricted. Adams urges a boycott of trade with the United Kingdom.

- 1775—Adams begins serving in the Second Continental Congress. He pleads for independence and union among the colonies. He is almost arrested by the British as he travels to Philadelphia.

- 1776—The Declaration of Independence is approved.

- 1780—Samuel Adams strongly supports article three of the Massachusetts Constitution. This article stated that members of various Christian denominations were to pay taxes to support their own churches. It also stated that non-church members and members of small religious minorities had to pay taxes to support the Congregational Church. This article remained law in Massachusetts until 1833.

- 1781—Adams is elected President of the Massachusetts Senate.

- 1784—Sam Adams is concerned about the lax morality in his beloved Boston. He makes it known that he is unhappy with the luxurious lifestyle and example set by John Hancock (he later becomes a political ally of Hancock). Adams opposes high fashion, gambling, and nightclubs that start to take root in the city. He writes about the need for citizens to return to the old Puritan virtues. He urges the people of Boston to break up the new *Sans Souci* nightclub with a mob if necessary. The club dissolves. Adams is accused of being a "baleful comet," a "son of sedition," a bigot, and a riot lover who would like to dictate the morals of the people.

- 1786—Adams opposes **Shays Rebellion.**

- 1787—While initially leaning against the ratification of the new Federal Constitution, Adams decides to support it *after he is convinced that amendments would be added later on to guarantee citizen's rights.*

- 1794—Adams soundly defeats the Federalist candidate and becomes Governor of Massachusetts. He supports the French Revolution and attends celebrations with French emissaries where "liberty, fraternity, and equality" are toasted.

- 1796—Samuel Adams runs as a presidential elector *opposed* to the candidacy of his cousin John Adams for President. John Adams becomes President. Samuel loses in his race for elector. He also announces that he will *not* run for re-election as Governor.

- 1803—Sam Adams dies.

Glossary

Committees of Correspondence—Committees in various American colonies that wrote to each other before and during the Revolutionary War. The first committee originated in Boston in 1772 at the suggestion of Samuel Adams. Their purpose was to uphold the rights of the American colonists and bring unity to the colonies in their struggle against England.

Congregationalism—A form of church organization where each local congregation governs its own affairs and calls its own ministers. These churches were dominant in early American New England.

East India Company—An English company that was chartered to conduct trade in the East Indies.

French and Indian War—The war fought on American soil between the British and the French for the domination of the North American continent. The war was fought during 1754-1763 and the British were victorious.

Intolerable Acts—Laws passed by the British Parliament that were intended to punish the people of Boston for their role in destroying tea in the *Boston Tea Party*. These laws closed Boston's port, required citizens to provide various goods to British soldiers, prohibited town meetings without the governor's permission, and provided that any British soldier arrested for murder could be sent back to England for trial.

Liberty Tree—A large elm tree in Boston that was used as a rallying point for the patriots.

Non-Importation—Agreements between various colonies or towns not to import English goods.

Oligarchy—a form of government in which the ruling power belongs to a small group of people connected by religious, social, family, or political ties.

Selectmen—Men elected to municipal offices in New England.

Theocracy—The rule of a state by those claiming to have the authority of God, His word, and His law.

THE HOLY EXPERIMENT
IN PENNSYLVANIA

In 1681, England's Charles II granted a charter to William Penn to govern the land of Pennsylvania. This was done to repay a debt that was owed by Charles to Penn's father who was an Admiral in the Royal Navy. Penn was a Quaker who was persecuted with other Quakers during the reign of the Stuart monarchs in England. He was imprisoned three times for his religious convictions. His first was in **The Tower** of London. While in this prison, he wrote the book *No Cross, No Crown* in 1668.

William Penn was well studied in theology, philosophy, and politics. Yet he believed in simple virtue and the uncomplicated teachings of Christ in the gospels. His thinking was shaped by the persecution that he saw being practiced by Protestant people who professed to be Christians. He and his Society of Friends (also called Quakers for supposedly "quaking" at some of their meetings) came out of the era of the English Civil Wars and the Puritan religious dissensions. The England of the mid-1600s had become a place where religious diversity expressed itself in such groups as the Anabaptists, Antiscripturists, Baptists, Brownists, Calvinists, Enthusiasts, Fifth-Monarchy Men, Independents, Perfectists, Presbyterians, Ranters, Seekers, and Socinians. Penn himself studied under Puritan theologian John Owen, but followed the religion of George Fox, the founder of the Religious Society of Friends. While the Quakers certainly departed from Puritan orthodoxy in religious matters, they went forward with such (Independent Puritan) ideals as religious toleration and the right of common men to have control over those who governed and taxed them. Penn passionately believed that no one should have their liberty or property taken away because of their religious beliefs, and he opposed religious coercion of any kind. He believed that religious persecution was caused by men of the clergy who had earthly desires and wanted power. His view was that the civil government should be concerned with civil matters and not religious questions.

Politically, Penn was a Whig who favored property rights and personal liberty. He knew the great history of English constitutional liberty. In his trial of 1670 for preaching without the government's approval, he appealed to the Magna Carta and the historical rights of English citizens under Common Law. However, he did not believe that personal liberty was a license to act immorally. Penn wrote in *An Address to Protestants* that "There can be no pretense of conscience to be drunk, to whore, to

be voluptuous, to gamble, to swear, to curse, to blaspheme, and [to be] profane....
These are sins against nature; and against government, as well as against the written
laws of God. They lay the ax to the root of human society."

In 1682, Penn came up the Delaware River into Pennsylvania, which means
Penn's Woods. Unlike the more unified Calvinist groups to the north and the
Anglican Church people in the south, he established a colony where people of all
Christian denominations were welcome to live, work, worship in their own
churches, and participate in the government. As Governor, Penn practiced peace and
fair trade with the Indians. He promoted **liberty of conscience** regarding religious
beliefs. He emphasized serving people in the spirit of the Christian gospel. The truly
remarkable thing about Penn was that he could have used his authority to enhance
his own personal power, but did not. Charles II gave him enough power to be a dictator, but Penn chose to voluntarily limit his own power, something rare in the history of politics. Penn wrote to the few existing settlers before he arrived, "I hope you
will not be troubled at your change, and the king's choice, for you are not at the
mercy of a governor that comes to make his fortune great; *you shall be governed by
laws of your own making, and live a free, and if you will, a sober and industrious people.*"
He also wrote to the Native Americans in Pennsylvania that he desired to gain their
"love and friendship by a kind, just, and peaceable life."

William Penn greets the natives of Pennsylvania

In 1682, he established the **Pennsylvania Frame of Government**. In the Preamble, Penn set forth his view that civil government is of divine origin. He quoted from the various epistles of the Apostle Paul to prove this. Penn believed that the purpose of government was twofold. First, it was to punish evildoers. Second, it was to reward those who lived righteously.

Penn made treaties with the Indians. He told them he met with them unarmed because he believed that the Great Spirit he worshipped disapproved of the use of force against his fellow men. He also *purchased* the land from them, something that he was not required to do in his charter from the king. Penn put the General Assembly in motion. A frame of government was established. In the second section of this body of laws, it was stated that every man might believe in any doctrine that was not destructive to the peace and honor of society; that every Christian man who was not a criminal could vote or be elected to the Assembly; that every child who reached age twelve should be instructed in some useful trade or skill; that legal fees should be fixed at a low rate and hung in every court of justice; that persons wrongly imprisoned should have double damages from the prosecutor; and that prisons should be changed into houses of industry, honesty, and education. The law allowed execution only for those guilty of willful and premeditated murder. The first session of the Pennsylvania Assembly lasted only three days, but laws of great importance were enacted.

Penn did not believe that the mechanics of government would ultimately safeguard the rights of the people. He stated in the preface to the *Pennsylvania Frame of Government* that, "Governments, like clocks, go from the motions that men give them; and as governments are made and moved by men, so by them they are ruined too. Wherefore governments rather depend on men, rather than men on governments. *Let men be good, and the government cannot be bad; and if it (the government) be bad, they will cure it. But, if men be bad, let the government be never so good, and they will endeavor to warp and spoil it to their way.*" Penn also stated, "Any government is free to the people under it where the laws rule and the people are party to those laws." The *Pennsylvania Frame of Government* was based upon the division of powers in government, and the rights of individuals in the colony.

In 1701, the **Charter of Privileges** was enacted. This was the second great charter of liberties that was associated with William Penn. When Penn returned to the Pennsylvania colony from England in 1699, he found that there were problems and people wanted political changes. The earlier *Pennsylvania Frame of Government* was repealed by 6/7 vote (as required), and the *Charter of Privileges* was put in its place. It provided for: freedom of religious belief, the right of accused criminals to have legal counsel and the right of calling witnesses in their favor, a General Assembly elected yearly, and the right of people to be tried before the judicial branch of government and not the executive. The Charter also stated that those who died by accident or committed suicide were to have their inheritance go to their families (and not be taken by the state).

William Penn brought to the colony a combination of peace, prosperity, and charity, which were all rooted in his conviction that these things were to be the results of people living the gospel. The colony of Pennsylvania was a model of religious toleration among the various sects of Christianity. The city of Philadelphia was founded and named by Penn. It is taken from the scriptures and in the Greek language means *brotherly love.*

Brief Biography

William Penn

♦ Oct. 14, 1644—Born, son of naval officer Admiral Sir William Penn.

♦ 1660—Enters Christ Church College (Oxford University). Penn opposes extravagant dress and behavior at the College. He also opposes, on religious grounds, the rule that everyone must attend the Church of England.

♦ Early to mid 1660s—Penn's father sends him to France, hoping that a fashionable life will make the young Penn forget his religious convictions.

- 1667—Penn goes to Ireland to manage his father's estates and becomes acquainted with Thomas Loe, a Quaker preacher. At age 22, Penn becomes a Quaker at a time when they are persecuted, ridiculed, imprisoned, and occasionally executed.

- 1668—Penn is imprisoned in *The Tower* of London for his religious beliefs and writes the book *No Cross, No Crown.*

- 1669—Penn is arrested again on charges of rioting and conspiracy.

- 1670—Penn is imprisoned a third time.

- March 4, 1681—Penn is granted a charter for land between New York and Maryland, which becomes *Pennsylvania* (or Penn's Woods). Charles II gives Penn this land to pay off a long-standing debt to Penn's father (a naval hero) after whom the land was named.

- 1682—William Penn establishes Philadelphia and the colony of Pennsylvania. He crafts the *Pennsylvania Frame of Government* as the law of the colony.

- 1684—He returns to England.

- Late 1680s—Penn is arrested under the rule of William and Mary, under suspicion of his friendship with James II. Later he is released and wrote two of his greatest works, *Some Fruits of Solitude* and *Essay Towards the Present and Future Peace of Europe (1693).*

- 1699—He returns to Pennsylvania to settle some troubles with slavery, piracy, and the government.

- 1701—The *Pennsylvania Charter of Privileges* is enacted. Penn later returns to London. He is falsely accused of debts and held in prison for a year. This imprisonment ruins his health.

- 1712—William Penn has a stroke that paralyzes him.

- 1718—William Penn dies.

Laws Agreed Upon in England by the Governor and Divers
of the Freemen of Pennsylvania. (This is the second section
of the Pennsylvania Frame of Government, 1682).
Some paraphrasing is included.

1. That all elections of representatives of the people...shall be free
    and voluntary: and if the elector [voter] shall receive any gift or
    reward such as food, drink, or money [to elect a candidate], he
    shall forfeit his right to elect [vote], and any person who gives such
    rewards to be elected shall forfeit his election.

4. That no money or goods shall be paid by any of the people [taxes],
    but by law which is made for that purpose; and whoever shall tax
    or collect contrary to law shall be held to be a public enemy to the
    province and a betrayer to the liberties of the people.

5. That all courts shall be open, and justice shall neither be sold,
    denied, or delayed.

6. That, in all courts, all persons may freely appear in their own way,
    and....personally plead their own cause themselves, or if unable to
    do so, by their own friends...

7. That all pleadings, processes, and records in courts shall be short
    and in English, and in an ordinary and plain character, that they
    may be understood, and justice rightly administered.

8. That all trials shall be by twelve men [juries], peers or equals, and
    of the neighborhood...

12. That all persons wrongfully imprisoned, or prosecuted at law, shall
    have double the damages against the informer, or the prosecutor.

17. That all fines shall be moderate, and not take men's merchandise,
    contentments, or wagons.

25. That the one-third of the estates of those who commit murder or
    treason shall go the next of kin to the one who suffered...

26. That all witnesses, called to testify in any court...shall give the truth, the whole truth, and nothing but the truth, to the matter in question. [If any] shall be convicted of willful falsehood, that person shall be punished in the same way as the person to whom he or she bore false witness against did, and shall make restitution to the person who was wronged, and shall be publicly exposed as a false witness, never to be credited in any court, or before any magistrate.

34. That all Treasurers, Judges, Sheriffs, Justices of the Peace, and other Officers in the government, and all members elected to serve in the General Assembly, and all who...elect them, shall be such as possess faith in Jesus Christ, and are not convicted of ill fame or dishonest conversation, and are twenty-one years of age...

35. That all persons living in this province, who confess and acknowledge the one Almighty and eternal God, to be the Creator, Upholder, and Ruler of the world, [who] live peaceably and justly in civil society, shall in no way be molested or prejudiced for their religious persuasion, or practice, in matters of faith and worship, nor shall they be compelled...to maintain any religious worship, place, or ministry whatever.

Glossary

Liberty of Conscience—The belief that people had the right to worship God according to the light of their conscience that God had given them, and that the government had no right to enforce religious doctrines or methods of worship. For the most part, this belief included Christians of all denominations but not necessarily people of completely different religions.

The Tower—A fortress on the Thames River in London that served as a prison in the 1600s. Many notable and courageous religious and political dissenters were sent there.

VIRGINIA

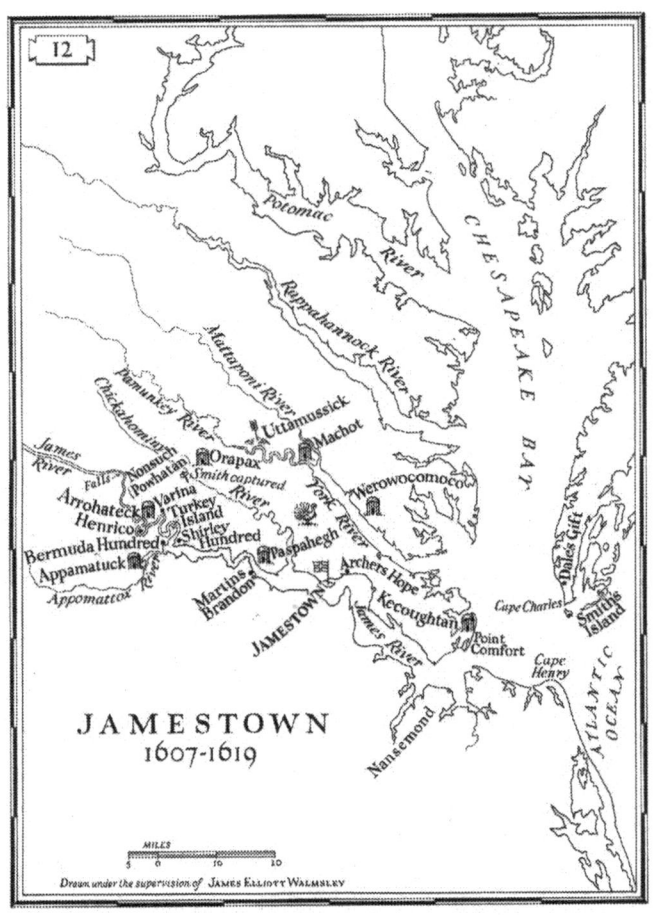

In 1607, English explorers landed in a swampy area near the mouth of the James River. Unlike the Pilgrims and Puritans who came to New England for religious purposes, these "Knights, Gentlemen, Merchants, and Adventurers" came mostly for economic reasons. In their charter, King James gave the settlers wide economic freedom, but he reserved the right to control any government that was established on American soil. This was to be done through a royal council established in London.

For over a decade the colony floundered. The marshy area they settled in caused sickness. Supplies from the homeland were poor. Trouble with the local Indian population was constant and the settlers were not able to fend off starvation. They also did not possess a strong work ethic. At least the reasonably effective leadership of the adventurous **Captain John Smith** kept the colony from ruin. He recognized one purpose of the colony to be "the erecting of the true religion among the Infidels (the natives), to the overthrow of superstition and idolatry." The colonists were not very successful in that enterprise. However, the noble ministry of Anglican minister **Robert Hunt** was inspiring. He preached, celebrated Communion, reconciled quarrels, and distinguished himself by his personal piety. He unfortunately died in less than two years.

After seeing good money being thrown after bad, investors in England demanded a re-organization. The king granted a new charter known as the Virginia Company. In 1609, five hundred men and one hundred women were sent over to re-populate and re-supply the colony. More bad times were to come. The vessel carrying the leaders was blown off course and wrecked in Bermuda. Disease was already breaking out among the settlers who landed in Virginia. Too weak to work at first, their social structure broke down and they fell into fighting, laziness, and despair. They did not plant the crops needed to survive the coming year, and they died in large numbers. When the winter of 1609-1610 was over, only 60 of the 500 inhabitants were still alive. In May, the previously shipwrecked leaders arrived from Bermuda and found utter desolation. Houses had been burned for wood. Cattle and domestic animals were all consumed for food. On June 7, the settlement was abandoned. But the departing settlers were met at the mouth of the James River by a longboat from a fleet that just arrived carrying 300 men and a new Governor, **Lord De la Warr.** The colony was re-established and social discipline was imposed in a code of laws entitled *Lawes Divine, Morall, and Martiall.* Compulsory service on common projects was enforced with severe penalties for those who would not work. Government by council was abolished and a one-man dictatorship under **Sir Thomas Dale** was established. Church attendance was mandatory. The law stipulated that a person could lose their provisions, be whipped, or even be executed for repeatedly missing divine services. Ministers who failed to do their duty were punished. Anyone who spoke against the Articles of the Christian Faith or the Trinity was to be put to death. However, the more severe penalties were not used. Some order was brought out of chaos and the colony began to prosper. Dale began the policy of allowing settlers to own stock in the Virginia Company. He also granted them individual plots of land to work for their own benefit.

Another important development was the realization by **John Rolfe** (who married the Native American Princess Pocahontas) in 1612 that tobacco could be grown for profit in Virginia. By 1617 tobacco was being planted in large quantities, even along the streets of Jamestown. In 1618, Sir Edwin Sandys took control of the Virginia Company from John Smith and developed a plan of generous land proposals for investors and settlers.

The most important development in Virginia was the grant of a representative assembly in 1619, the first government in America. Later, in 1622 a great disaster struck. The local Indians, deprived of their lands and terrorized by some Englishmen, attacked a string of defenseless farms along the James River and massacred 347 people. The colonists responded by taking up arms at the expense of planting crops. A bloody reprisal took place along with famine.

In eighteen years, only about one-sixth of the colony's 8500 souls actually survived this misery and deprivation. In 1624, James I decided to revoke The Virginia Company's charter by court action. In most ways, the colony was a failure. But in one way it was a success. An elementary practice of the rule of law and colonial self-government was established in America. Virginia then became a royal province with direct rule by the governor who was appointed by the king. However, the old representative assembly was still retained. This assembly, known as the House of Burgesses and acting as a lower house, had the authority to enact laws that were not contrary to the laws of England, but whose legislation was still subject to veto by the king. The Anglican Church was established as the official religion of the colony, although Puritan sympathies ran high in both the church and the colony.

In 1676, **Bacon's Rebellion** stung the territory. Because of high taxes, economic hardship, and the failure of **Governor Berkeley** to prosecute the Indian war aggressively, some colonists rose up under **Nathaniel Bacon.** He marched his supporters into Jamestown, and they gained control of the House of Burgesses through force. Governor Berkeley fled to the Eastern shore of the Chesapeake. However, the rebellion was soon over as Bacon died of dysentery later that year. The aged Governor Berkeley was restored to power and hung 23 rebel leaders. **Charles II** thought that this retribution was excessive and recalled him to England. When it was all over, *Bacon's Rebellion* was a forerunner of the American Revolution.

One enduring aspect of the settlement was **The First Charter of Virginia** of 1606. *In this document, the colonists were understood to have the rights and liberties of Englishmen.*

In the 1700s, Virginians developed both strong ties to the Crown and deep affection for English liberty. They also became concerned about laws passed by the Parliament that they believed were a violation of their rights. They wanted real representation in the English government if they were to be taxed. By the 1760s and 1770s, western, upcountry men of Virginia like **Thomas Jefferson** and **Patrick Henry** were leading the way toward the assertion of their rights as Englishmen, and eventually towards independence. At the Second Virginia Convention on March 23, 1775, Patrick Henry gave his most eloquent speech at St. John's Church in Richmond. He asked, " Is life so dear or peace so sweet as to be purchased at the price of chains and slavery? Forbid it, Almighty God! I know not what course others may take, but as for me, give me liberty or give me death!" In this discourse, he alluded to the *First Charter of Virginia.*

Virginia's **Declaration of Rights,** written primarily by George Mason, became one of the models for the Bill of Rights to the U.S. Constitution. Adopted on June 29, 1776, *it became the first American Bill of Rights established by an American state.* This happened a few days before independence was declared. It was done through an elected convention. Mason was an uneducated planter who had very little legal training. Yet he composed the Virginia Bill of Rights upon his general knowledge of political theory. Mason did not invent these rights. *A consensus had already developed among the leaders of the American Revolution that government had a duty to protect people's fundamental rights.* Mason simply wrote down those accepted ideas.

Excerpts from The Virginia Declaration of Rights, 1776

1. That all power is vested in, and consequently derived from, the People; that magistrates are their trustees and servants, and at all times amenable to them.

5. That the Legislative and Executive powers of the State should be separate and distinct from the Judicial...ought to be free, and that all men, having sufficient evidence of permanent common interest with the community, have the right of suffrage [to vote], and cannot be taxed or deprived of their property for public use without their own consent or that of their Representative so elected, nor shall they be bound by any law to which they have not....agreed to, for the public good.

7. That all power of suspending laws, or the execution of laws, by any authority, without consent of the Representatives of the people, is injurious to their rights, and ought not to be exercised.

8. That in all capital or criminal prosecutions a man has a right to demand the cause and nature of his accusation, to be confronted with the accusers and witnesses, to call for evidence in his favor, and to a speedy trial by an impartial jury of his vicinage [neighborhood], without whose unanimous consent he cannot be found guilty, nor can he be compelled to give evidence against himself; that no man may be deprived of his liberty except by the law of the land or the judgment of his peers.

9. That general warrants, where an officer may be commanded to search suspected places without evidence of a fact committed, or to seize any person(s) not named, or whose offense is not particularly described and supported by evidence, are grievous and oppressive, and ought not to be granted.

12. That the freedom of the Press is one of the greatest bulwarks of liberty, and can never be restrained but by despotic governments.

13. That a well-regulated Militia, composed of the body of the people, trained to arms, is the proper, natural, and safe defense of a free State; that standing armies, in time of peace, should be avoided as dangerous to liberty; and that, in all cases, the military should be under strict subordination to, and governed by, the civil power.

16. That Religion, or the duty which we owe to our Creator....can be directed only by reason and conviction, not by force or violence; and therefore, all men are equally entitled to the free exercise of religion, according to the dictates of conscience; and that it is the mutual duty of all to practice Christian forbearance, love, and charity, towards each other.

THE GREAT DEBATE

After America won her independence, she muddled around for a half-decade or so in debt and uncertainty. Many people thought the **Articles of Confederation** was too weak to govern the country. A **Constitutional Convention** was called and fifty-five delegates from all the states went to Philadelphia (except Rhode Island, which refused to have anything to do with the revision of the Articles). Patrick Henry and Richard Henry Lee of Virginia refused to attend the convention, even though they were selected by their legislature to do so. Henry said, "I smell a rat." Samuel Adams of Boston was ill, and did not attend. Jefferson and John Adams were serving abroad as ministers of state, and also unable to go to the convention.

James Madison took the lead in a new proposal for a government. It was not a revision of the *Articles* he wanted but a "systematic change" of government. The radical **Virginia Plan** was to provide for a national republic that was to replace the independent republics of the various states. In the new republic, **John Jay** said that the states would stand in relation to the national government in the same way that counties stand to the states. Most of the delegates knew that a substantial increase in power was going to go to the federal government in such areas as taxation and the regulation of commerce. But some of the delegates wanted to maintain the basic sovereignty of the states.

Opponents of the nationalists came up with a plan of their own called the **New Jersey Plan** (delegate William Paterson of New Jersey introduced it). This plan was more of an amendment to the *Articles of Confederation* than a destruction of it. So with the Virginia and New Jersey plans on the table for debate, a crisis loomed on the horizon.

In the end, the **Connecticut Compromise**, led by **Roger Sherman**, won the day. Although the national legislature was not given the power to veto state laws that were passed, it was given power to levy tariffs (import taxes), coin money, borrow money, and regulate commerce between the states. There would be one national currency and no more taxes imposed by one state on another when goods were shipped between them. The Convention decided on a strong chief executive (the President) with power over the armed forces, the authority to direct diplomatic relations, and the power to appoint people to the executive and judicial branches of government. He was to be elected to office by electors chosen from the states and equal to the number of the Representatives and Senators from each state. The Virginia Plan's suggestion to have a federal judiciary whose judges would hold office "during good behavior" (essentially for life) was accepted without dispute. The Senate would be composed of two Senators from each state who would be appointed by that state's legislature, although Madison and Wilson originally wanted them to be elected in proportion to the population. The House of Representatives was to be the democratic branch of government in which representatives would be elected by the people and sent to the Congress in numbers proportionate to the state's population. The federal Constitution was sent to the states for their ratification. This was to be done not by state legislatures, but by specially elected state conventions. Only nine of the thirteen states (2/3) had to ratify it. The Anti-federalists objected to this.

The new Constitution *also lacked a bill of rights.* Alexander Hamilton and James Madison believed that a bill of rights was unnecessary since the Constitution carefully limited the powers of the new government. Anti-federalists, including Virginia's George Mason, Patrick Henry, and James Monroe opposed the new Constitution. They thought that too much power was granted to a central government. They also opposed the Constitution because it had no bill of rights. On September 12, 1787, Elbridge Gerry of Massachusetts introduced a motion to "appoint a committee to prepare a Bill of Rights." George Mason of Virginia actually inspired this motion. He had stated that his desire was to see the Constitution prefaced by a bill of rights. This motion was unanimously defeated by the states (which voted as units). Most of the delegates felt that the Declarations of Rights by the various states were good enough to protect the people. They believed that the new federal government was not given any power to infringe on the rights of the citizens. Charles Pinkney of South Carolina made a proposal guaranteeing freedom of the press and the right of citizens not to have soldiers stationed in their homes during peacetime. It added that, "the military shall always be subordinate to the civil power".... This was also defeated by the convention unanimously. The Constitution was approved *without* a bill of rights, and after the hottest summer in memory, the convention adjourned on September 17.

When the Constitution went to the states for ratification, approval was in doubt. Rhode Island was hostile. North Carolina steadfastly refused to ratify until a bill of rights was added. Virginia and New York experienced long and strenuous debates. However, by March 4, 1789, the Constitution was ratified by eleven of thirteen states. Rhode Island and North Carolina jumped on board within a year.

Even as they voted to ratify, Virginia, New York, and Massachusetts all proposed amendments to the new federal document. George Mason took the lead in opposing the Constitution by stating that the individual state's Bills of Rights were not good enough. He urged the states to reject it unless a federal bill of rights was added. Four other men were in the forefront of the Anti-federalist cause. They were Elbridge Gerry of Massachusetts, Richard Henry Lee and Patrick Henry of Virginia, and Luther Martin of Maryland.

Richard Henry Lee's *Letters from the Federal Farmer* was one of the most effective arguments against the Constitution. In Letter number five, he urged the states to alter and amend the system before they adopted it. Luther Martin was a leading lawyer and a dissenting member of the Constitutional Convention. He wanted a bill of rights added during the convention. When this failed, he wanted to see it added by the states during their deliberations on approval.

In a 1788 letter of *Brutus* (a pseudonym used by a Massachusetts Anti-federalist), it was written that the federal government needed to make sure that the rights of those accused of a crime were protected. Brutus gave his opinion that since the various states had bills of rights making sure that no one could be compelled to be a witness against himself, had to see his accusers face to face, and had to have a trial in his or her vicinity; the federal government needed to have the same rights established in its Constitution. He said, "What security is there, that a man shall be furnished with a full and plain description of the charges against him? That he shall be allowed to produce all the proof he can in his favor? That he shall see the witnesses against him face to face, or that he shall be fully heard in his own defense by himself or counsel?" He concluded rather harshly that, "persons who attempt to persuade people that such reservations (to the Constitution) were less necessary under the Constitution than under those of the States, *are willfully endeavoring to deceive you, and lead you into an absolute state of vassalage* (emphasis added).

More writings came forth from *Agrippa* (probably a pseudonym for James Winthrop). In a January 14, 1788 treatise, he went so far as to call the Philadelphia Constitutional Convention a "treasonable conspiracy." He also lamented the lack of a bill of rights in the new Constitution. In February of the same year, he proposed that the Constitution be accepted *only* with fourteen conditions he set forth. Most of these did not have to do with a bill of rights *per say*, they were mostly restrictions placed on the activities of the federal government. They did not become part of the Constitution.

George Mason of Virginia objected to the proposed Constitution as lacking a declaration of rights. He believed that the House of Representatives had the *shadow* of representation, but not the *substance*. Mason believed that the Senate was constructed with too much power, which would "enable them to accomplish what usurpations they please, upon the rights and liberties of the people." He further stated, "The judiciary of the United States is so constructed and extended, as to absorb and destroy the judiciaries of the several states; thereby rendering laws tedious, intricate, and expensive, and justice as unattainable by a great part of the community, as in England; and enabling the rich to oppress and ruin the poor."

Most importantly, Mason observed that Congress may "inflict unusual and severe punishments" and *there is no declaration of any kind for preserving the liberty of the press, the trial by jury in civil cases, nor against the danger of standing armies in time of peace."* He did say in a letter to George Washington later that year that he favored sending the proposed Constitution (even with his objections) to a convention of the people in each of their states for a vote on ratification.

The Federalists did not take things lying down. They mounted a massive campaign to combat the objections of the Anti-federalists. One of the chief defenders of the Constitution *without* a bill of rights was **James Wilson** of Pennsylvania, possibly one of the best lawyers in the new nation. He staunchly defended the view that whatever power was *not* given to the Federal Government was *reserved* (held back from it), making a bill of rights unnecessary.

In an address to a meeting of the citizens of Philadelphia in 1787, Wilson argued that in the case of freedom of the press, no power of control over the press was given to the federal government in the Constitution, therefore no special right protecting the press was needed. He also explained that while *state* governments operated on the principle that power not kept from the states was automatically *given to* them, the Federal Government was to operate differently. It was to operate on the basis that power not explicitly given to it was to be withheld from it (reserved). In Wilson's opinion there was no need to establish this in a separate bill of rights. Some of the Anti-federalists did not want a standing army in time of peace and Wilson attacked this idea as unworkable and jeopardizing the security of the new nation. He addressed the concern that the Senate would become an aristocracy by saying that it was chained on two sides. One side was that on legislative matters, the Senate had to have the agreement of the House of Representatives; on the other side concerning its executive powers (approval of treaties and federal judges), it had to work with the President.

Wilson even claimed that some opponents of the Constitution weren't interested in protecting the liberties of the country, but were opposed to it because their wealth and consequences might be upset.

James Sullivan wrote another letter under the surname **Cassius.** In defense of the Constitution, he stated that since the House of Representatives directly answered to the people of their districts, no bill of rights was necessary. He argued that if the people's representatives could by-pass answering their constituents, they could also by-pass a bill of rights. In his letter, he called the Anti-federalist writer *Agrippa* a numbskull and said that the Anti-federalists were knaves, blockheads, and the *opposition junto.* He accused them of opposing the Constitution on irrational grounds. Cassius came to the conclusion by asking that his countrymen not "listen to the mad dictates of men, who are aiming at every artifice and falsehood, which the emissaries of hell can invent, to effect your total destruction and overthrow." Cassius described the Anti-federalists as people "who wish to ascend the chariot of anarchy, and ride triumphant over your smoking ruins, which they hope to effect, by their more hellish arts: in your misery they hope to glory, and establish their own greatness on their country's ruin."

Letters of a Countryman, written by Roger Sherman of Connecticut, was also a defense of the Constitution without a bill of rights. He opened by mentioning the "impertinence and folly with which the newspaper politicians (Anti-federalists) have overwhelmed many parts of our country." Sherman stated, "The only real security that you can have for all your important rights must be in the nature of your government. If you let any man govern you who is not strongly interested in supporting your privileges, you will certainly lose them." He commented that, "No bill of rights ever yet bound the supreme power (of government) longer than the honeymoon of a new married couple." His view was that since his own state had a legislature that could change the people's rights with new laws every year (even *with* a bill of rights), the Federal legislature could do the same thing *without* a bill of rights. The issue for Sherman was not a bill of rights, but the election of representatives that would properly safeguard the rights of the people. He admitted that there was enough authority given to the House of Representatives "to do the greatest injury." Yet he believed that if the people had control over the federal legislature, their rights would be safeguarded because that body would represent their interests. The questions for him were, "How is Congress to be formed?" and, "How far have you a control over them?" To decide these two questions was far more important for Roger Sherman than a bill of rights.

The best and most classic defense of the Constitution *without* a bill of rights came from Alexander Hamilton, who wrote under the surname of **Publius.** In *The Federalist* (written by Hamilton, Madison, and Jay) No. 84, Hamilton echoed the idea that the people reserved (or possessed) all rights that were not mentioned in the Constitution. He even thought that a bill of rights would be dangerous because whatever rights were *not* mentioned in it could quickly become controlled or prohibited by the government. He questioned, "Why declare that things shall not be done which there is no power (by the government) to do?" Hamilton's view was that the *Magna Carta* and the *English Bill of Rights* were primarily tools that were used against monarchies. He reasoned, "They have no application to constitutions professedly founded upon the power of the people, and executed by their immediate representatives and servants." He stated that the Preamble to the Constitution (We the People…) was a better recognition of human rights than all the bills of rights in the various state constitutions. Hamilton stated that a bill of rights "would sound much better in a treatise of ethics than in a constitution of government."

On March 4th, 1789, the new Constitution was ratified by eleven of the thirteen states *without* a bill of rights. Rhode Island and North Carolina signed it in about a year. However, the influence of the Anti-federalists (and Thomas Jefferson) was strong enough to get James Madison to commit to working for a bill of rights shortly after the ratification of the Constitution. In the summer of 1791, the House of Representatives approved seventeen amendments to the Constitution. The Senate reduced these to twelve. Two were dropped when the list was referred to the states. The ten amendments, now called **The Bill of Rights**, were ratified by three-fourths of the states and became part of the Constitution in December of 1791.

Brief Biography

Patrick Henry

- May 29th, 1736—Patrick Henry is born in Hanover County, VA.

- As a young boy, he is educated by his father.

- At age fifteen, Henry becomes a storekeeper. He went into heavy debt by granting too much credit. Within a year, he and his brother liquidate the business.

- In 1757, fire destroys Henry's home and belongings. He sells most of his slaves and uses the money to buy another country store.

- The second store fails. Henry again cannot (or will not) collect from those on credit.

- Patrick Henry helps run his father-in-law's tavern. He earns a reputation for hospitality.

- April 1760—He leaves the tavern business and arrives in Williamsburg for a law exam. Though not well studied, he passes the exam with three votes for and one against.

- During the 1760s, Henry takes on a large volume of cases and becomes a successful lawyer.

- In a famous case called "the Parson's Cause," Henry becomes famous for his oratory. In this trial, he opposes both the British Crown and the established Anglican Church.

- In 1765, Hanover County leaders send him to fill a vacant seat in the Virginia House of Burgesses. During this time he opposes the Stamp Act. In his speech, he is accused of treason and replies, " If this be treason, make the most of it."

- During the late 1760s and early 1770s, Henry acquires huge amounts of land and a significant number of slaves.

- 1774—Henry oversees the formation of the Hanover County militia. His wife also goes insane and is taken care of by a slave in the basement of his mansion. She dies in 1775.

- March 23, 1775—Patrick Henry gives his most famous speech at St. John's Church in Richmond. As the Virginia House of Burgesses listens, he thunders with his legendary golden tongue, "Give me liberty, or give me death."

- 1775—Patrick Henry serves in the Continental Congress without distinction.

- 1776—He resigns his post as Commander-in-Chief of Virginia's army.

- Later in 1776, he becomes Governor of the new Commonwealth of Virginia. He successfully recruits soldiers for the militia and the Continental Army. His state also sends cattle to feed Washington's troops at Valley Forge.

- 1788—Serving in the Virginia State Convention as an Anti-federalist, Patrick Henry opposes the ratification of the U.S. Constitution. He does this on the grounds that it endangers the rights of individuals and states, and that the document lacks a bill of rights for the people's protection. He is also concerned that Virginia's western border will not be protected by a new national government. During the 1780s, Henry opposes Jefferson and Madison on a number of issues. Thomas Jefferson greatly dislikes Henry, even though they agree on the need for a bill of rights.

- Late in his career—Patrick Henry becomes a Federalist. In 1796, he is elected Governor of Virginia but refuses to accept the job. Later, he was elected to the Virginia State Legislature, but he died before his term began.

Glossary

Articles of Confederation—The agreement in which the 13 original colonies established the first government of the United States in 1781. The document guaranteed the sovereignty of each state and each state had one vote in Congress regardless of its size and population.

Connecticut Compromise—The plan from Connecticut's delegates to the Constitutional Convention that proposed the form of federal government that was made the law of the nation. It was a compromise of both the Virginia and New Jersey Plans. It established a lower House where bills to raise revenue were to be started and the people directly elected the representatives in proportion to the population. It also established a Senate where each state was to send two members that were elected by that state's legislature.

Constitutional Convention—The meeting of delegates from various states in 1787 to establish a new Constitution for the United States. This group of men abandoned the *Articles of Confederation* to form the Constitution because they believed *The Articles* were too weak to govern the nation. The Convention was held in Philadelphia and its delegates agreed to deliberate in secret.

New Jersey Plan—Plan for the Constitution that called for a unicameral legislature (one body), each state having one vote, and a President and Vice-President elected by the Congress.

Virginia Plan—Written mostly by James Madison, this plan for the Constitution called for a bicameral legislature (lower and upper houses) in which the lower house elected the upper house and the people elected the lower one. In this plan, the lower house would elect the President and federal Judges.

POSTSCRIPT

You may ask the question, "Does the Bill of Rights contain *all* of man's God-given rights in the political sense?" Some would say *yes*, the essentials are covered. Others would say *no*, the concept of human rights grows with time because new rights may not have been realized yet.

It is important to remember that the Bill of Rights has to be understood in light of the ancient English and colonial documents that have been explained in this book.

Life, liberty, and personal property were the main concerns of those who gave us the Bill of Rights. Those who fought for the Bill of Rights in our Constitution believed that since God granted these rights to human beings, it was the duty of civil government to protect the people in their possession of these rights. They especially did not want to see the government shed innocent blood or punish people unjustly with the law. This is why we have the right to a trial by jury. It is also why we have the right to a speedy trial, and the right to compel (force) witnesses to testify in court. Every accused person in our country has the right to an attorney for their defense, even at taxpayer expense if they can't afford it. **Remember, tyranny comes in many forms,** *including the tyranny of law.*

There has been a lot of debate in this country over the last 30 or 40 years regarding the issue of gun ownership. Do individual citizens have the right to keep and bear arms or does this right belong only to an organized militia? People may always argue whether or not it is morally acceptable for citizens to own or carry guns. There are well-meaning ideas on both sides of this issue.

James Madison, who wrote the Second Amendment, and Richard Henry Lee, made it plain that they intended the word "militia" in the Second Amendment to mean an armed populace, not military reserve units. They both denounced the Prussian style militias that were under the control of the government. The Second Amendment came from the belief that a large standing army (in time of peace) was a threat to the nation. Many of the founders wanted state militias to defend the nation from foreign attack *and* to defend their territory from the federal army if necessary. Lee wrote that, "to preserve liberty, it is essential that the whole body of the people always possess arms." A *well-regulated* militia was what the Bill of Rights called for, not a militia *controlled by* the federal government. The idea at our nation's beginning was that the militia was to be composed of physically capable males with their own weapons acting in the common defense. Does this need to change? If it does, then another amendment to the constitution is needed.

What about the concept of "privacy rights?" The Fourth Amendment to the Constitution is very clear: **The right of the people to be secure in their persons, houses, papers, and effects, against unreasonable searches and seizures, shall not be violated....** The issue of privacy is tied to the property that people own. While there is no right to privacy to commit criminal acts (even if done in private), there is a clear right to privacy regarding one's personal possessions. This is something that has to be safeguarded especially in our day of computer technology where both government and private industry can easily snoop on citizens and violate their rights.

The right of individuals to keep their property, documents, possessions, and personal effects free from *arbitrary* search or seizure by the government is essential if a society of free people is to continue. Remember, only probable cause and a search warrant issued by a judge allow the police to search or take someone's private possessions. Also, our perception of privacy can never be used to take away someone else's civil rights. *The Fourth Amendment does not give us the right to possess illegal things in secret, or commit criminal acts in secret.*

Our Bill of Rights in the United States Constitution specifically defines rights such as freedom of the press, a public and speedy trial, freedom of religion, and the right to keep personal possessions private. *In these first ten amendments to the Constitution, the people's rights are held up as more important than the rights of government officials.* The Bill of Rights has a noble history that goes all the way back to the Magna Carta. You have read in this book about the roles that bishops, kings, soldiers, politicians, ministers, lawyers, and common people have played in the development of our rights. Time, human struggle, and God's providence have woven these rights into the fabric of our society. Our Bill of Rights has wonderfully laid down these protections that are based on the moral laws of our Creator. We must not lose them, and we must avoid inventing "rights" that really don't exist.

BIBLIOGRAPHY

Amos, Gary, *Defending the Declaration*—Wolgemuth & Hyatt Publishers, Inc. 1989

Bailyn, Bernard; Davis, David; Donald, David Herbert; Thomas, John L.; Wiebe, Robert H.; Wood, Gordon S.—*The Great Republic*—Little, Brown, & Co. 1977

Beeman, Richard R.—*Patrick Henry, A Biography*—McGraw Hill Book Co. 1974

Beliles, Mark and McDowell, Stephen—*America's Providential History*—Providence Press 1989

Bolles, Albert S.—*Pennsylvania, Province and State*—Burt Franklin Publishing 1970 (Reprint)

Burns, Edward McNall; Lerner, Robert E.; Meacham, Standish—*Western Civilizations*—W.W. Norton & Co. 1980 (9th Edition)

Calvin, John—*On God and Political Duty*—(Edited by John T. McNeill)—The Bobbs-Merrill Company, Inc. 1950, 1956

Cantor, Norman F.—*The English, A History of Politics and Society to 1760*—Simon and Schuster 1967

Cantor, Norman F.—*Western Civilization, Its Genesis and Destiny, Volume 1*—Scott, Foresman, and Co. 1969

Churchill, Winston—*History of the English Speaking Peoples, Volume 1*—Dodd, Mead, & Co. 1958

Churchill, Winston—*History of the English Speaking Peoples, Volume 2*—Dodd, Mead, & Co. 1965

Crow, Herman and Turnbull, William—*American History, A Problems Approach*—Holt, Rinehart, and Winston, Inc. 1971

Donnelly, John P.—*Faith of Our Fathers, Volume 2*—McGrath Publishing 1977

Faulkner, Harold Underwood—*American Political and Social History*—Appleton, Century, Crofts 1957

Forbes, Esther—*Paul Revere and the World He Lived In*—Houghton Mifflin Co. 1942

Johnson, Paul—*A History of the American People*—Harper Collins 1997

Miller, John C.—*Sam Adams, Pioneer in Propaganda*—Stanford University Press 1936

Morris, Richard B. and the Editors of Time Life Books—*The New World/Before 1775*—Time Life Books 1963

Schwartz, Bernard—*The Bill of Rights, Volume 1*—Chelsea Hill Publishers in association with McGraw Hill 1971

Wallace, Dewey Jr.—*Faith of Our Fathers, Volume 3*—McGrath Publishing 1977

Historical Image Credits

ABOUT THE AUTHOR

John Patterson has been involved in local politics, social concerns, religious work, and radio broadcasting for over twenty years. He was a Township Commissioner and a radio commentator in the Pittsburgh area, and has spoken at a variety of forums on politics, religion, history, and education.

INDEX

0-595-31398-1

www.ingramcontent.com/pod-product-compliance
Lightning Source LLC
Chambersburg PA
CBHW031233280526
45784CB00004B/1558